Towns and Cities in the Great War

Dover

in the Great War

Towns and Cities in the Great War

Dover

in the Great War

Stephen Wynn

First published in Great Britain in 2017 by
PEN & SWORD MILITARY
an imprint of
Pen and Sword Books Ltd
47 Church Street
Barnsley
South Yorkshire S70 2AS

ISBN 978 1 47382 793 6

Printed and bound in England by
CPI Group (UK) Ltd, Croydon, CR0 4YY

Pen & Sword Books Ltd incorporates the imprints of Pen & Sword
Archaeology, Atlas, Aviation, Battleground, Discovery, Family
History, History, Maritime, Military, Naval, Politics, Railways,
Select, Social History, Transport, True Crime, and Claymore Press,
Frontline Books, Leo Cooper, Praetorian Press, Remember When,
Seaforth Publishing and Wharncliffe.

For a complete list of Pen and Sword titles please contact
Pen and Sword Books Limited
47 Church Street, Barnsley, South Yorkshire, S70 2AS, England
E-mail: enquiries@pen-and-sword.co.uk
Website: www.pen-and-sword.co.uk

Contents

About the Author

Stephen is a retired Police officer having served with Essex Police as a constable for thirty years between 1983 and 2013. He is married to Tanya and has two sons, Luke and Ross, and a daughter, Aimee. His sons served five tours of Afghanistan between 2008 and 2013 and both were injured. This led to the publication of his first book, *Two Sons in a Warzone – Afghanistan: The True Story of a Father's Conflict*, published in October 2010.

Both Stephen's grandfathers served in and survived the First World War, one with the Royal Irish Rifles, the other in the Mercantile Marine, whilst his father was a member of the Royal Army Ordnance Corps during the Second World War.

Stephen collaborated with Ken Porter on a previous book published in August 2012, German PoW Camp 266 – Langdon Hills. It spent six weeks as the number one best-selling book in Waterstones, Basildon between March and April 2013. They have also collaborated on other books in this local history series.

Stephen has also co-written three crime thrillers which were published between 2010 and 2012, and centre round a fictional detective named Terry Danvers. *Dover in the Great War* is one of numerous books which he has written for Pen & Sword in the *Towns and Cities of the Great War* series which commemorates the sacrifices made by young men up and down the country.

CHAPTER ONE

A brief history of Dover and why the war took place

The fact that the First World War actually started was not a shock to most serious observers of the day; it had always been a case of when rather than if. This was because most countries had been making plans for war for many years, not with a view to necessarily starting one, but for how best to defend themselves when it eventually arrived. By the turn of the twentieth century the chances of a war not taking place were really quite low. With all of the political and military posturing that had been going on, coupled with the number of treaties that were in place amongst countries trying to protect themselves from the threat posed by powerful neighbours, it was never going to take too much in the way of an incident to ignite the political powder keg that was waiting to explode upon the world.

So it was that the assassination of Archduke Franz Ferdinand on 28 June 1914 in Sarajevo, Serbia, began what became known as the Great War.

It would be more than four years before normality would once again descend on mankind. The real shock of those times came in the scale of its brutality and senseless waste of human life, which were on an almost industrial scale. Never before had the world experienced such a maelstrom of its own design and making.

What was Dover's part in all of this madness? Let us take a look, but first a brief history of the town and what it was like at the outbreak of the First World War.

Dover has an important and historical past, mainly due to its position on the Channel coast and the existence of its castle, which has seen many changes over the centuries. If its inner walls could talk, they would have many a tale to tell. Although there had been fortifications in Dover since before the Battle of Hastings in 1066, it was only during the reign of King Henry II, between 1133 and 1189, that today's Dover Castle really began to take shape.

In 1216 King Louis Vlll of France, with the support of some disloyal English barons, tried his best to take the castle and with it the English Crown, but failed after being unable to breech the castle walls.

It played a prominent part during the English Civil War between 1642 and 1651, when during the first year of the war it was captured from the king's supporters by the Parliamentarians. The war saw the eventual demise of both King Charles I and an eventual victory for the Parliamentarians at the Battle of Worcester on 3 September 1651.

The Napoleonic wars of the early nineteenth century saw Dover become a garrison town, with barracks being added to the inner sanctum of the castle's defences as part of massive improvements, overseen by William Twiss, a renowned military engineer. One way or another the town of Dover has had a prominent role to play over the years in the history of England.

Dover Market Square

CHAPTER TWO

1914 – Outbreak of War

At the end of July 1914, as the spark that ignited the flames of the First World War was struck in Sarajevo, the 6th and 8th Destroyer Flotillas of the British Royal Navy were engaged in a military exercise in the Straits of Dover. After it was over they arrived at Dover harbour on 26 July, along with three scout cruisers, HMS *Pathfinder*, HMS *Adventurer* and HMS *Attentive*.

The next day the *Attentive*, whilst still in Dover harbour, fired her guns and ran up the Blue Peter, which is the nautical name for

Dover Harbour

a signal flag (P). It is raised when a ship is about to leave port, and it is a warning to all crew members of that ship to get back on board immediately.

Within the hour HMS *Pathfinder* and a number of destroyers left the harbour and made their way up the east coast of England, possibly to Harwich. In the meantime the activity in and around Dover was really starting to be ramped up. The town's residents knew something was going on; they couldn't but know, they had heard the two loud bangs from the direction of Dover harbour and, after realizing that neither was an explosion, most would have worked out what had in fact happened, even if they didn't know exactly which ship had fired the shots. Later the same day a train arrived from Portsmouth. It was packed with enough sailors to make the crews of both the *Adventurer* and *Attentive* up to war strength.

Seeing so many men suddenly coming into the town after what had happened at Dover harbour earlier the same day, still wouldn't have necessarily caused a panic in the minds of those townsfolk aware of international tensions. The declaration of war by Great Britain against Germany was still some nine days away and the threat to Belgium had not yet taken place. Most would have believed that another training exercise was underway.

On 26 July with the military situation throughout Europe getting worse by the minute, Britain attempted to organize a conference to look at the dispute between Serbia and the Austro-Hungarian Empire, the reason behind why Europe was close to the brink of a war, to see if these matters could be resolved by political means. This included most of the major European powers. France, Russia and Italy all agreed to the conference but Germany, who by now seemed hell bent on going to war, refused to attend.

On the evening of 27 July HMS *Hazard*, a Submarine Depot ship, arrived at Dover in company with several C Class Submarines; their arrival could have been simply more vessels that were due to take part in the supposed training exercise.

The situation in Europe quickly deteriorated and on 28 July Austria-Hungary declared war on Serbia, bringing the threat of an all-out European war even closer.

The British Government, which was still trying to do all that it could to prevent war, called for international mediation on 29 July, but alas, it did not materialize. On the same day, Russia, becoming increasingly concerned about Germany's intentions, begins a mobilization of her troops as a precautionary measure. Germany immediately follows suit and begins to mobilize.

The next day, 30 July, saw HMS *Bulwark* arrive at Dover harbour with HMS *Arrogant* in tow. *Arrogant* became the stationary flagship at Dover for the Port Admirals as well a home and sleeping quarters for the submarine crews from the 4th and 5th Submarine Flotillas who used the port throughout the war. From February 1918 she became one of the ships of the Dover Patrol until the end of the war.

The activity of naval ships arriving and leaving Dover harbour, kept on increasing. On 31 July, eleven Tribal-class destroyers arrived including HMS *Alfrida, Amazon, Cossack, Crusader, Gurkha, Maori, Mohawk, Saracen, Tartar, Viking* and *Zulu.*

The likelihood of war increased with the passing of each day. The Port of Dover had searchlights added to its defensive capability for the first time, and during the hours of darkness they would continuously sweep backwards and forwards across the harbour basin, paying particular attention to the entrances. Across the English Channel the outbreak of war was getting closer to becoming a reality as Germany declared war on Russia, and France and Belgium began the full mobilization of their troops.

Monday, 3 August 1914 was a Bank Holiday throughout England and Wales, which was the excuse for most to make their way to the coast and enjoy some leisure time. The weather was mainly cool and slightly unsettled for the first few days of the month, but it was good enough for the traditional Bank Holiday Monday cricket matches of Surrey v Nottinghamshire at the Oval and Lancashire v Yorkshire at Old Trafford to take place. It was also the day that the Foreign Secretary, Sir Edward Grey, remarked whilst watching the street lights being lit that evening outside his office in Whitehall, 'The lamps are going out all over Europe. We shall not see them lit again in our life time.'

Rumours of naval battles being heard in the North Sea were rife amongst those sitting upon the white cliffs of Dover. Some were under the misapprehension that the war had already begun. Some may have been there in the hope that they might witness some action between the British and German fleets.

This was the day that Germany declared war on France. The following day Great Britain declared war on Germany and a dark cloud settled over Europe that brought with it death and destruction on an industrial scale. It would be more than four years before sanity and peace returned.

In what was a last minute attempt to escape an all-conquering German army, Britons and Belgians clambered aboard all available ships leaving the Belgian ports and headed for England. The last ship to make it out of Belgium before Britain declared war on Germany was the *Princess Henriette*, a paddle steamer which sailed out of Ostend with over 1,200 people on board and arrived at Dover on 3 August 1914. She had been launched on 14 March 1888, having been built by William Denny & Brothers in Dumbarton on the River Clyde for the Belgian government, and during the war she served as a troopship based at Folkestone, sailing backwards and forwards across the English Channel.

Her arrival at Dover was watched by Lord Kitchener who was waiting to leave for Calais on his way back to Egypt when he received a telegram offering him the vacant position of the Secretary of State for War. He changed his plans and returned to London the same day to take up the post.

Princess Henriette Paddle Steamer

The *Princess Henriette* survived the war, having taken thousands of soldiers across the English Channel to fight in France and Belgium, and was eventually scrapped in 1922.

The day that Great Britain declared war on Germany for refusing to recognize Belgium's neutrality and remove her troops, was a busy one with all of the last minute political ramifications that were taking place to try and prevent war. The sailing of the Dover to Calais passenger ferry was suspended with immediate effect and a British destroyer captured two German merchant vessels in the English Channel and escorted them into Dover harbour. They were the *Franz Horn* and the *Perkeo*. Their crews were removed and initially taken to Archcliffe Fort, off Bulwark Street in the town. During the war the Fort was the home to 3rd Fortress Company, Royal Engineers. The *Franz Horn* was sold at auction in 1915 to Melrose Abbey Shipping and renamed the *Melrose Abbey*.

J.B. Firth's book, *Dover and the Great War*, explains that the last passenger ship to arrive at Dover from Calais before war broke out was the SS *Endgadine* with a mere twenty passengers on board, whilst the last one to arrive from Ostend was the Belgium-owned *Rapide*, with over 1,000 passengers. Amazingly, as soon as she had off loaded her passengers, she returned to Ostend with six passengers, who, knowing the political and military situation in Belgium at that time, must have desperately wanted to make the journey.

The Dover to Ostend crossing did not resume until 18 January 1919, when the *Ville de Liege* sailed with 332 passengers on board, nearly all of whom were Belgian exiles returning to their country. Her full capacity at that time was 900. During the war she had served both as a troop carrier and a hospital ship between England and France.

The tightness of the security in and around Dover had increased as war drew closer. Notices were put up all round the town warning residents that they should not approach any military establishments or sentries, especially during the hours of darkness, and if they did they were to immediately obey any instructions given by any military personnel who were present.

In addition certain roads in the town had been closed including the old St Margaret's Road as well as the Old Dover – Folkestone Road which had been closed between Aycliffe House and Abbotscliffe

House. There were similar restrictions placed on some of the paths that run along the cliffs. Swingate Downs was an area designated as being out of bounds to the public, possibly because of the airfield that had been put in place there.

At the outbreak of war the Dover Garrison consisted of the King's Own (Royal Lancaster Regiment), the Lancashire Fusiliers and the Royal Inniskilling Fusiliers, which were all part of the British Army's 12th Infantry Brigade. Collectively they all left Dover on 8 August 1914, initially for a location on the east coast of England before leaving for France, most arriving there on 22 August. Their commander was Brigadier General H.F.M. Wilson, who had previously been in charge of the Dover Command.

Just four days after arriving in France, the 12th Infantry Division, part of the British Expeditionary Force (BEF), were involved in the Battle of Le Cateau during the retreat from Mons. In total there were 40,000 British troops involved in the battle, 7,812 of whom became casualties, out of these 700 were killed. Another 2,600 were taken prisoner.

Of the three regiments that had been part of the Dover Garrison and who had left the town on 8 August, 200 were killed in the fighting at Le Cateau. This included ninety-nine men from the Lancashire Fusiliers, sixty-six from the King's Own (Royal Lancaster Regiment) and thirty-five from the Royal Inniskilling Fusiliers. Many of those who were killed had no known grave and their names are commemorated on the La Ferté-Sous-Jouarre Memorial, in the Seine-et-Marne region of France.

The dead included Lieutenant Colonel Alfred McNair Dykes, of the 1st Battalion, King's Own (Royal Lancaster Regiment), who had served in the 2nd Boer War in South Africa, between 1899 and 1902.

The Dover Garrison was eventually replaced by the 5th and 6th Battalions, Royal Fusiliers (City of London) Regiment, who were stationed at the Duke of York's School. The 3rd East Surreys and the 3rd Buffs (East Kent Regiment) were at the Citadel. The 3rd Battalion, Royal Sussex Regiment were at Connaught Barracks and the 4th Battalion, Royal Sussex Regiment, had the luxury of being garrisoned at Dover Castle.

With the beginning of the war an unusual calmness prevailed

amongst the people of Dover. But was that so surprising, after all it was a garrison town with at least four separate regiments garrisoned there at any one time? There was also a strong naval presence, which included the respected Dover Patrol. The actual fighting on the ground in France and Belgium was far enough away across the Channel for it still not to feel totally real, especially as the hundreds of thousands of men who would be wounded during the course of the war had not yet started arriving back in the UK. Air attacks by German Zeppelins and Gotha bombers had not yet begun, so the potential threat to public safety from them, had not even been considered.

At the beginning of the war, there was no fear of a German invasion in the minds of the public, but that did not stop the authorities from preparing for that eventuality. A system of field defences were put in place around Dover, to make it as secure as it could be and a designated military area. The work was carried out by a civilian labour force.

Dover Castle was a natural choice for the headquarters of this new designated area, not just because of its location and prominence within the town, but because with its heavy artillery guns, it had more than sufficient fire power and capability to be able to protect Dover Harbour as well as the Straits. It was also tasked with monitoring the numerous shipping movements, in and out of the harbour, both merchant and military alike.

On 14 August 1914, Dover had another well-known military figure arrive in town, in the shape of General Sir John French, who was the Commander-in-Chief of the British Expeditionary Force. He was on his way to Boulogne on board the British Navy vessel, HMS *Sentinel*.

The *Sentinel* was a cruiser, originally launched on 19 April 1904. At the outbreak of the war, she was being used as a scout for the 6th Destroyer Flotilla and based at Dover. She survived the war, ending her days as a mechanics' training ship at Chatham, between 1920 and 1922.

Sir John French was a man of Kent, born literally just up the road in the neighbouring town of Deal.

In the early days and weeks of the war the German Fleet did not venture out into the

General Sir John Denton Pinkstone French

HMS Sentinel

English Channel, which allowed the Royal Navy to deploy submarines, destroyers and other vessels in the Dover Straits. Initially the British decided against deploying any mines in the Straits, so as to enable vessels from neutral countries safe passage.

To assist with the safety of shipping in the Straits, British airships, or dirigibles as they were also known, both the Silver King and the Astra-Torres classes, conducted sea patrols. Interestingly, whilst they were on land and not flying, their protection was in part in the hands of Dover's Boy Scouts, who were being utilized so as to allow military personnel to be employed on more important duties. At the outbreak of the war the British reportedly only had three airships in total, and two of these were operating from Dover.

Once the war had started in earnest, everybody wanted to do their bit for the war effort in whichever way that they could. Benevolent organizations sprang up to assist the hundreds of men who poured into the town, as well as all the local men, who were called up for military service. It wasn't just the comfort and care of the soldiers and sailors that these local organizations looked to help, some even catered for their friends and families as well. The Dover Corporation opened up Maison Dieu as a rest place for the families of men undergoing military training in the area. Today the medieval building is part of the old Dover Town Hall buildings.

One of the issues the war brought with it very early on was that of refugees, which in the main were from Belgium. The people of Dover were warm and welcoming to those who arrived in the town and fully appreciated their plight. Between 10 and 17 October 1914, somewhere in the region of 8,000 Belgian refugees arrived at Dover to escape from the ever advancing German army. Most arrived on passenger vessels, whilst others, including women and children, used whatever means they could. There were literally hundreds who arrived in small fishing boats, so desperate were they to escape. There were also 5,000 wounded Belgian soldiers who were dispersed to hospitals in and around Dover as well as other parts of Kent.

Refugees arriving in such large numbers were a headache for the British military authorities, who were concerned that amongst their numbers might be one or two German spies who had seized the opportunity to slip into England undetected. With Dover being one of the most important military locations throughout the United Kingdom, it was only right that such concerns were raised.

Brigadier General Fiennes Henry Crampton took up his new position as Officer in Command of the South Eastern Coast Defences on 4 January 1914, and by all accounts he was not impressed with the state of what he discovered, deeming that the defences were far from adequate. In the early weeks of the war he issued an order excluding all foreigners from Dover, living or visiting. By the end of November 1914 there were only three still present in Dover, and then only because they had been given special permission to remain. Soon after this Dover was declared a special military area open to only those who needed to be in the town. Even then anybody attempting to enter either by rail, or road, could only do so if they were in possession of a special pass.

HMS *Pathfinder* was a Pathfinder class of scout cruiser, which was destroyed on 5 September 1914, off the coast of St Abb's Head in Berwickshire, when it became the first ship to be sunk by a locomotive-type torpedo fired from a submarine. This type of weapon is self-propelled and is designed to detonate on impact or in close proximity to its target. The German submarine in question was U-21, commanded by Kapitänleutnant Otto Hersing. The *Pathfinder* sank within a matter of minutes after an initial large explosion, which indicates that that the torpedo struck one of the ship's magazines. Out of a crew of 289 officers and men, 259 perished.

U-21 sank a total of forty Allied ships during the First World War, the *Pathfinder* being the first of them, and damaged another two. In the seven days between 16 February and 22 February 1917, she sank thirteen Allied ships, eight of those on 22 February. She survived the war and was accidently sunk in the North Sea whilst under tow en route to Britain on 22 February 1919.

This was how the people of Dover and the surrounding areas heard the news that Great Britain had declared war on Germany. This announcement appeared in the edition of the *Dover Express* newspaper dated Friday, 7 August 1914. Not as you might think on the front cover of the newspaper as would seem fitting for such a momentous occasion, but on page five which, when taking into account that the paper in its entirety was only eight pages, appears to be somewhat out of proportion to the importance of the news it was reporting. Little did the people of Dover know that it would be more than four years before they received the news that the war was finally over.

Here are just a few relevant stories taken from the first wartime edition of the *Dover Express*.

Boom Defences at Dover Harbour

'The Commander-in-Chief at the Nore asks us to give publicity to the fact the Boom Defences at Dover are placed, with a view to the same being more generally known to local ship owners and seamen.

In another column are published full details of the procedure necessary to be observed as regards entering the Port. During the night or fog it is forbidden to enter the Port, and during the day-time special regulations as to examination have to be complied with. Vessels wishing to enter have to await outside the Port until the arrival of the examination steamer, which service is being carried out by the "Lady Crundall" and the "Lady Brassey" tugs.'

These restrictions would have particularly affected the local fishing industry, whose hours of working were governed by the times of the tides. But in a time of war, needs must, which most people would have no doubt understood.

The internal waterways of the port, as well as the approaches, were patrolled by naval patrol boats and captains and masters of merchant vessels, as well as any person who was in charge of a barge, or a boat of any kind. They had to observe any orders given to them by the Navy patrols. All such vessels were subject to an inspection and search, and would be liable to be fired upon should they fail to observe orders given to them by a naval patrol boat. Any vessels wishing to enter the port had to proceed to one of the Examination Anchorages outside the port and drop anchor, unless they had previously been met by the Examination Steamer. The Western Examination Anchorage was west of the Admiralty Pier, and the Eastern Examination Anchorage was east of the eastern arm of the breakwater. Any vessel proceeding between the two anchorage points had to keep one mile outside of the entrance to the port until they were past Dover. Once at anchorage, vessels were not allowed to leave that location under any circumstances, nor were they allowed to communicate with any other shipping or with anybody inland without having previously obtained permission from the Chief Examining Officer.

No vessels were allowed to be underway within the confines of Dover harbour during the hours of darkness except with special permission of the King's harbour-master, and in the case of fog, all movement by any vessel was absolutely forbidden. No merchant or private vessels were allowed to leave the Dockyard Port of Dover during the hours of darkness or whilst it was foggy, and no vessels were allowed to leave the without the permission of the Collector of Customs, at Customs House Quay in Dover.

Merchant ships or private vessels were not allowed to approach any kind of government vessel or dockyard without special permission. Although merchant vessels were allowed to navigate as usual within the confines of the Port of Dover, they had to keep clear of His Majesty's ships which were being navigated within the same location. A boom defence was in position across the entrance to the port and had to be approached with extreme caution. The gate of the boom was always closed during the hours of darkness or when it was foggy and also during the day when it was deemed necessary to do so. When it was open there were signals clearly visible on either side of the entrance wall to the Port of Dover, to indicate to all vessels who had the right of way.

Deserter who wished to rejoin

With the war only a day old there was the unusual case of the deserter who had re-discovered his desire to serve his king and country and handed himself into the authorities.

Frederick George Strong was a private in the Royal Marine Light Infantry, attached to HMS *Forth* when he deserted on 5 July 1913 whilst the vessel was lying up at Devonport Dockyard in Plymouth. Since then he had been living with his wife in Margate, but on the outbreak of war he decided that he had to return to his ship. He sent his wife back to live in Plymouth and then walked to Dover to locate his ship, but to no avail, so he decided to hand himself in to the Police. At 5.35pm on 5 August, Strong walked in to Dover Police station and handed himself in, explaining to Sergeant Pierce that he was a deserter.

The following day Strong appeared at the Dover Police Court, before Messrs H.F. Edwin and F.W. Prescott, where he was charged, on his own admission, of being a deserter. He was remanded to Canterbury to await instructions from the Admiralty as to what should be done with him.

Dover and the War

With the outbreak of the war, there understandably came a certain amount of uncertainty and worry about just exactly what was going to happen and how this would ultimately affect the lives of local people. To try and put their minds at rest and to stop any kind of panic, the Mayor of Dover, Mr E.W.T. Farley and the Fortress (of Dover) Commander, Brigadier General F.H. Crampton, issued the following notice:

Take Notice
'Those who are desirous of rendering services to their country and their fellow townsmen at the present time are particularly requested to show a strict observance of the following.

(1) Only such gold as is absolutely necessary should be drawn from the Banks. Paper money, such as cheques and notes, along with silver, should be used as far as possible.

(2) Provisions should not be purchased in greater quantities than usual. A shortage is unlikely. The control of the import of food stuffs is in military charge and consignments receive preferential treatment on the Railways.

(3) Panic or alarm are unnecessary, and all signs of them should be avoided. Dover is unlikely to be attacked whilst there is a British Fleet on the Sea.

God save the King
(6th day of August 1914).

A particularly interesting paragraph appeared in the edition of the *Dover Express* newspaper, dated 7 August 1914. It commented that the war against Germany had begun less than three days before and already the town had seen changes. The daily cross-Channel passenger ferries that plied their trade between Dover and France had already ceased to operate, but still the town remained as the frontier post of the country, and the nearest place in all of England to German soil.

The war was seen as a just cause in a battle of good over evil, right over wrong, with a loss of honour and integrity if it had not been pursued. The desire was for a short war that would result in a victorious peace for Britain and her allies, a reasonable expectation for most people, and one that was achievable by universal self-sacrifice, not only by the people of Dover, but by everybody throughout the entire country.

The nation needed the young men of Dover to do the right thing for their country and enlist in the armed forces, and those who remained behind also had to do their bit and go steadily about their business so that there was as little disruption as possible to trade and industry.

With the onset of the war came a relatively new phenomenon, that of panic buying in relation to food and provisions. Many of the shops in Dover had experienced this 'absurd' practice, which although good for business was not so good for the wellbeing of the townspeople as it risked unfair price increases. As there was no expectation in the early days of the war that it would last for more than four years, there was also a belief that there was not the least chance of the Germans interfering with merchant ships that were full of food and on their way to Great Britain.

The newspaper article ended with two final points. The first was in relation to restrictions on the Press and what they could and could not report. With the outbreak of the war came the Defence of the Realm Act, or to give it its more popular acronym, DORA. This legislation provided the government and the military with wide-reaching powers that allowed them to do basically whatever they saw fit to do for what they saw as the safety of the country. There had not been too much detail provided in the press about the specifics of certain elements of Britain's preparation for war. This was a balance between a nation's morale and its people's need to know, against the risk of providing an enemy with too much information.

Lastly, there was a reference to both Lord Kitchener's appointment at the War Office and the successful work at the Admiralty being carried out by Winston Churchill which somehow conjured up the belief that as a result of their joint efforts and abilities, the war would be over in just a matter of a few short weeks and that peace would once again return to the world.

War Episodes at Dover
Captures of German Shipping

'The first episodes beyond the mobilization scenes that occurred at Dover were the capture on Wednesday about noon of two German vessels. The first capture was that of a fine four masted barque. The "Perkoe", (late "Brilliant") 3,765 tons, from New York to Hamburg, with oil. She is very similar in many respects to the wrecked "Preussen". She came up Channel under full sail, but the appearance of one of the destroyers at Dover compelled her to shorten her sail and heave to. The tide and wind, however, carried her a good way towards St Margaret's before she was towed back by the tug into Dover Harbour, and subsequently, her fine appearance proved one of the sights all the afternoon for the crowds on the Sea Front. Another capture, almost simultaneously, was that of the steamer "Franz Horn," of Lubeck, which was hauled up and brought in to the Harbour, and it, though less conspicuous, proved a valuable prize. The crews have been removed as prisoners of war.'

With the war underway the harbour at Dover became an extremely busy location and making sure a record was kept of all comings and goings of ships and other vessels, was imperative. Besides naval vessels, fishing boats, large ships bringing food and other essential items into the harbour, there were also passenger vessels arriving from Belgium with refugees which greatly added to the confusion.

Newspapers provide numerous accounts of bravery by soldiers who had fought and died whilst serving their king and country. There were also accounts of other war-related incidents and activities which took place within Dover that are worthy of repeating in these pages.

Private Downham of the 6th Battalion, Royal Fusiliers, who was stationed at Dover Castle, received a commendation from his commanding officer for his gallant conduct in saving the life of a woman who was bathing in the sea at St Margaret's Bay on 19 August 1914. The unnamed woman was out of her depth and at real risk of drowning until Private Downham intervened by wading into the sea and plucking her from the water. In carrying out this unselfish act he injured himself by 'straining his heart' and, having pulled the lady to safety, had to be assisted ashore by one of his own colleagues and taken to the local hospital, where he was detained for further treatment.

His commanding officer commented that 'he looked forward to Private Downham setting the same example on the battlefield as in peace.'

Saturday, 22 August 1914 saw an enthusiastic recruiting meeting take place at Dover Town Hall. Prior to the meeting the band of the 5th Battalion, Sussex Regiment played patriotic songs at the nearby Granville Gardens, before setting off for the town, playing as they went, and assembling in the Maison Dieu Hall where they gave a stirring rendition of the music to the 'Veteran's Song'. The meeting was presided over by the Mayor of Dover, Councillor E.W.T Farley with other local dignitaries and senior military officers in attendance, including Brigadier General F.H. Crampton, the Fortress Commander at Dover and Colonel Wyndham who, as well as being responsible for organizing the town's recruitment for Kitchener's New Army, was also the brother of the late Member of Parliament for Dover.

The Mayor addressed those present, which included a large number of women who had ensconced themselves in the Town Hall's upper galleries. He started off by telling everybody that the meeting was a call to arms to the young men of Dover. His personal belief was that every able-bodied, single young man in the town should be willing to enlist and want to serve their king and country in a true show of patriotism. His own nephew had enlisted in the Lancers just the previous week.

He reminded the audience that now was not a time for playing cricket, golf or tennis and that those leisurely pastimes should be put to one side so that men could hold a rifle to their shoulder and go and fight for their Empire. He knew and understood that the war would bring great suffering not only to the men who would go off and fight, but to the women who were left behind, be they mothers, wives, daughters or sisters, but especially the mothers who had given birth to the very sons who would now go off and fight. He called upon them to have the noble courage to give freely of their sons, so that they in turn could do their duty and answer the call in their thousands, and in doing so show to the world that the spirit of men from the Cinque Ports was alive and well and that if need be they would lay down their lives for the defence of their country. With the coming of the war one of the greatest yet bloodiest battles that had ever been fought was about to take place and that history was in the making; he wondered what part the young men of Dover were going to play in it.

Others who made speeches at the meeting were Brigadier General Crampton, Colonel Sir Montague Bradley and Colonel Wyndham, whilst Lieutenant Colonel F.G. Hayward of the Dover Field Artillery said that he needed fifty-eight recruits to bring the brigade up to

Men signing up for Active Service Battery of the Dover RFA

strength and he hoped that as a result of the meeting he would get those recruits by the middle of the following week. He explained that the brigade would need men for both home defence and foreign service, but he was quick to point out that he did not wish to push the needs of his brigade above that of Lord Kitchener's army.

The edition of the *Dover Express* dated 18 September 1914 included an article about the death of a well-known Dover man who had been killed in fighting on the Western Front. The news was all the more tragic as the man's father had died unexpectedly the previous year.

Death of the late Mr G. Wyndham's son

'It will be with the deepest regret that Dover will learn that the Hon. Percy Wyndham, son of the late Mr G. Wyndham, has been killed at the Front. He was in the Coldstream Guards, and his death has not yet been officially announced, but the sad news was communicated to his relatives. The Hon. Percy Wyndham is half-brother to the Duke of Westminster, Countess Beauchamp (the wife of Lord Warden of the Cinque Ports), and Lady Shaftesbury. He was the only child of the late Mr G. Wyndham, born in 1887, and was married last year to Miss Diana Lister, youngest daughter of Lord Ribblesdale, and a niece of Mrs Asquith. The tragic death of Mr G. Wyndham in Paris last year, followed by the death of his son so soon, is a terrible blow to Countess Grosvenor, and the deepest sympathy is felt for her.'

According to the Commonwealth War Graves Commission website 26-year-old Percy Lyulph Wyndham, was a lieutenant in the 3rd Battalion, Coldstream Guards and was killed in action at Soupir during fighting at the Battle of the Aisne on 14 September 1914. He was 26 years old. He has no known grave and his name is commemorated on the memorial at the La Ferté-Sous-Jouarre, in the Seine-et-Marne region of France. The memorial contains the names of 3,740 officers and men who were killed at the battles of Mons, Le Cateau, the Marne and the Aisne, during a six-week period between August and October 1914.

At the time of Percy's death, his mother, Countess Grosvenor, was living at 35 Park Lane, London, having been born at Tickhill Castle in Yorkshire. With Percy away in the war, and living on her own, the Countess was looked after by eight servants. By May 1921, she had moved to Paighton Grange in Cheshire.

In his will, Percy left £179,003 17s 5d, to George Henry Drummond, Esquire.

In early October 1914 the decision was taken to raise a Dover Anti-Aircraft Searchlight Corps. The conditions of service were as follows:

(1) Enlist for the duration of the War.
(2) The members of the Corps will be granted commissions, uniforms, and ratings in the Royal Naval Volunteer Reserve.
(3) Night work only on alternate nights.
(4) Approximate numbers required 120.
(5) Good general health, eyesight and hearing essential; no age limit.
(6) Apply at the Town Hall Friday or Saturday, 9 and 10 October, between 6 and 10 pm; and Monday 12 October, between 6 and 8 pm.

The following were some of the names of local men that were submitted to the Admiralty for approval to be accepted into the Corps: Lieutenant Commander Dr Ian Howden, Lieutenant Commander Instructor H.D. Capper; Sub Lieutenants, Captain J.R. Clarke, Colonel Charles Hardy, Mr Travers B. Harby, Mr H.H. Vasse, Mr W.T. Rust, Mr H.N. Hoare; Control Officers 2nd Grade, Messrs J.M. Barnard, C.E. Beaufoy, E.M. Birch, G.F. Chandler, E.E. Chitty, F. Clayton, P.A. Cockburn, J.J. Cullinane, H.R. Geddes, H.H. Goodwin, J.W. Harvie, V.P. Martin, G.M. Norman, G.G. Redfern, F. Ridgen, G. Thomas, B.G. Turner, P.G. Wraith; Control Officer for General Superintendent, Mr H. Teesdale.

The phrase, 'It'll all be over by Christmas', was often bandied about in the early months of the war, but sadly the war was still going on at Christmas 1914.

Mr Nelson and Mrs Eliza Hannah Whiteman of 18 Buckland Avenue, Dover, received a letter from Captain R. McGillycuddy of B Squadron, 4th Battalion, Dragoon Guards, informing her of the death of her son, Sergeant (D/3258) Evelyn Guy Whiteman, on 6 September 1914. He was 24 years of age and a single man. The letter read:

'Mrs Whiteman,

It is with deep regret that I have to inform you of the death of your son who was killed in action on September 6th, 1914, at Pecy.

He was struck by a shell when advancing in the firing line and died three minutes later in the arms of my Squadron Sergeant Major, never regaining consciousness. He was buried by the comrades of his own squadron, at the above named place, who deeply deplore his loss and desire to express their sincere sympathy. I have forwarded his personal effects to you.

R. McGillycuddy
Captain, 4th Dragoon Guards'

Sergeant Whiteman is buried at the Perreuse Chateau Franco British National Cemetery, which contains the graves of a total of 150 Allied servicemen from the First World War, who were initially buried elsewhere and brought to the cemetery after the end of the war.

Jessie Ada Hall was a widow who lived at 52 Maison Dieu Road in Dover. Her husband, Francis Marshall Hall, had died some years before, leaving her with four young children to bring up on her own: a daughter, Milba, and three sons, Francis, Marshall and Bernard. In early September Mrs Hall received a letter informing her that one of her sons, Bernard, who was a drummer with the 2nd Battalion, Suffolk Regiment, had been killed during fierce fighting at the Battle of Le Cateau on 26 August. After having spent two weeks mourning his sad demise, she then received news that he was in fact not dead after all, but very much alive, and had been taken prisoner by the Germans.

It all started on 25 September, when another of Mrs Hall's sons, who lived in Felixstowe, received news from a comrade of Bernard's, that he had been killed in action on 26 August. Understandably, and in all good faith, he informed his mother of what he had been told. Mrs Hall then wrote to Bernard's regiment enquiring of them if they had any news about what had happened to him. She received a reply informing her that he was officially listed as being 'missing'. She spent the next two weeks trying to take in the enormity of the situation, then received a letter dated 6 October. It was from one of her son's friends, Drummer Jones, who was with him during the fighting at Le Cateau, informing her that Bernard hadn't been killed but had been taken prisoner with other men from their battalion. The relief felt by Mrs Hall on reading that letter, can only be guessed at. To add to her joy on 25 October she received a card with a German post mark written by her son, in which he informed her that he was safe and well and not to worry about him.

After the war Bernard went out to India to work for the Imperial Tobacco Company which was situated in Ghandi Ghowk, Delhi, in India. On 29 September 1924 he married Constance Thurzia Pannell, who was 18 years of age, in Cawnpore, Bengal, India. Her father, Alfred Archer Pannell, had served with the Royal Artillery for more than twenty-two years, between 29 November 1897 and 31 August 1920.

Bernard Hall left Tilbury on board the SS *Egypt* on 19 May 1922 en route to Bombay, stopping off at Marseilles. The crew numbered 294 whilst there were only 44 passengers on board the ship when it left Tilbury. Most of her passengers would be joining them when the ship docked at Marseilles. Her cargo included £1,054,000 in gold and silver. On the evening of 23 May 1922, the *Egypt* was sailing in thick fog off of Ushant. Captain Collyer heard the sound of another ship's whistle, but due to the worsening weather, he was unable to locate it. A short while later she was struck by the French cargo steamer *Seine* and within twenty minutes she had sunk beneath the waves.

During the First World War the *Egypt* was commandeered by the Royal Navy, painted white, marked with a red cross and used as a

P&O Steam Navigation Company's SS Egypt

hospital ship. Fifty members of the crew as well as thirty passengers are believed to have been killed, but Bernard Hall was one of the lucky ones who survived, although he lost his war time medals in the sinking and had to apply for replacement ones, a request which was granted.

A letter appeared in the *Dover Express*, of 8 January 1915, dated 26 December 1914. It was from Private R. Tapley of the 10th Field Ambulance C Section, Royal Army Medical Corps. It read as follows:

'Dear Sir,

Thinking that you might like to know how Christmas was spent by members of the Field Ambulance, I thought I would write a few lines trying to give a brief description of the events. At 9.30am we were paraded and each man received from the Officer Commanding a Christmas card from the King and Queen and also a card from the officers of the Fourth Division.

In the morning, which was intensely cold, we enjoyed a good game of football, followed by dinner, comprised of tinned stew and Christmas pudding, which we thoroughly enjoyed. I might mention that the puddings were from the "London Daily News Fund". After dinner an impromptu concert was held at our main dressing station, presided over by the Officer Commanding. It was very successful, and with the help of a couple of barrels of best Belgian beer and some English cigarettes sent by some kind friends in dear old England, we were made very comfortable. I might add that the concert was held in the main hall of a deserted convent, and there were very plain marks everywhere to show that it had suffered severely from the bombardment of the Germans. Everywhere was to be seen great gashes in the walls caused by pieces of shell, and I think I can safely say that hardly a window remained.

After we had been sent up in the evening to make sure that there were no more cases to come down, we gave a concert at our station, which was attended by both officers. Again with the help of good beer and cigarettes and an exceedingly good programme, a happy evening ensued. This was held in a barn, and we borrowed a piano, which we fetched from a villager's in one of our ambulances. Considering circumstances, I think every one thoroughly enjoyed themselves.'

In the British Army Pension Records for 1914 – 1920, I found a Private 7481 Frank Herbert Reginald Tapley, who was a member of the 10th Field Ambulance, Royal Army Medical Corps, who had arrived in France on 23 August 1914, and whose home address was 39 Council House Street, Dover. I would suggest that this is the letter writer.

In the 1911 Census Frank's mother, Lilly, is shown as being single and visiting an address in Lewisham, London, whilst a 15-year-old Frank was living with his step-sister and her husband along with his two younger sisters, at the Royal Hotel in Dover.

Before the war he worked for the Union Castle Line, as a ship's steward in the Merchant Seaman Service. He enlisted in the Royal Army Medical Corps on 6 January 1914 at Whitehall in London, and first arrived in France less than three weeks after the start of the war. He was there for some fifteen months before moving on to Belgium, Salonika, Malta, Egypt and Palestine. It would also appear that he could speak German as he was used as an interpreter. In June 1916 he contracted malaria and spent time at the 28th General Hospital in Salonika during June and July 1916 and another hospital in Malta between July and November 1916.

After the war he was placed on the Army Reserve on 18 March 1919 in Blackpool. At the time his wife, Mrs L. Tapley, was shown as living at 11 Oakley Terrace, Maxton, Dover, Kent.

The German naval attacks which took place at Scarborough, Hartlepool and Whitby on 16 December 1914 showed that the war in Europe could arrive on the mainland of Great Britain. With German Zeppelins and Gotha aircraft regularly taking part in bombing raids over the next few years, having to deal with such bombardments from the skies was going to become more and more commonplace, so knowing what to do in those situations would become extremely important for the civilian population.

Fortunately for Dovorians there was little chance in the early months of the war of the Germans landing an armed force in their midst, but there would be every chance of a seabourne artillery bombardment, as there had been on the north east coastal towns. The attack by ships of the German Imperial Navy resulted in 137 civilian deaths and 592 casualties. During the attack, over 1,000 shells rained down on the communities of Hartlepool, Scarborough and Whitby, damaging nearly 300 homes, seven churches and five hotels.

It was discovered from the attack that the safest thing to do was to stay indoors and take shelter in either basements or cellars, and window shutters should be closed where possible to reduce the risk of injury from flying glass.

The Vice Lieutenant of Kent took the opportunity to inform everybody that the recent security measures that had been taken and the notices that had been sent out to people, were only of a precautionary nature and emphasized the fact that a hostile landing by German forces was not expected, and in fact, it was highly unlikely, but the measures had been implemented because there was a possibility.

With the emergency committees, the local military authority and the Police all working closely with each other, they thereby ensured the most effective possible resistance to the Germans should they either attempt or succeed in making a landing on the English coastline.

CHAPTER THREE

1915 – Deepening Conflict

The following letter by someone signing himself A. Patriot, was sent to the editor of the *Dover Express* and printed in the edition of the newspaper dated 29 January 1915:

'Sir,

As there are many of our inhabitants who are capable, but refrain from assisting the Nation during the existing struggle with our enemies, either by enlisting in the New Army or becoming a member of our Local Volunteer Corps, it will be most unfair and unpatriotic if these slackers are permitted to slide through the period of stress in full security and without effort of any kind and in many cases also without contributing one penny towards the heavy cost of the War.

It is well known that several eligible men without encumbrance are still dormant and have no intention of even making themselves efficient for home defence, and unless enforced, will make no attempt to assist. For such who are apparently afraid of their skins, I would suggest they should contribute towards the cost of those who are combating the enemy and protecting our shores. This could be systematically carried out by debiting the War Tax on property to the tenants, thereby increasing the rent by the amount of Tax. If the principal property owners arrange such a procedure it would give those eligible men the choice either to serve their country or contribute towards the cost of those who

*volunteer. Perhaps other readers will endorse this suggestion or
at least state their views.'*

A letter written by somebody who had possibly suffered in some way
either directly or indirectly as a result of the war, or perhaps a property
owner who wanted rents to be raised for their own benefit?

The editor replied in the following terms:

> *'This looks like a scheme to raise rents. There are extremely few
> cases where the course suggested would touch a "shirker", but
> the introduction of the system would make things harder for many
> with diminished incomes, owing to husbands having enlisted and
> prices having increased without justification. We do not see how
> there is any patriotism in shifting a war property owners' tax on
> to tenants.'*

Friday, 18 March 1915 saw a story in the *Dover Express* about a
prisoner of war from Dover. His name was Corporal Ernest S. Datlen
(2391) of the 9th Battalion Queen's Royal Lancers. He had arrived in
France on 15 August 1914 as part of the British Expeditionary Force
and sustained a shrapnel wound at the Battle of Mons where he was
taken prisoner. He was sent to a prisoner of war camp in Doeberitz in
Germany where he survived the war.

An interesting letter appeared in the *Dover Express* on 23 April.
It was written by Colonel C.A. Mercer (Retired), the Commanding
Officer of the 11th Kent (Dover) Battalion of the National Reserve:

> *'Sir,*
> *It has occurred to me that our Dover citizens would be interested
> to know how many men belonging to the 11th Kent (Dover)
> Battalion of the National Reserve have re-joined the Colours
> since the beginning of the war, and I have therefore much
> pleasure in forwarding a nominal roll of the men with the units
> to which they now belong, and shall feel greatly obliged by your
> publishing the same in your next issue. There is every reason to
> believe that many others have responded to their country's call
> to arms, of whom we have so far heard nothing. It is also very
> gratifying to know that at least twenty-eight members of Classes
> II and III of the Battalion, whose business, profession or callings*

could not admit of their taking up Military or Naval Service, have joined the Dover Volunteer Training Corps.

The aspirations of a large number of men of Class III, who are willing and eager to serve their country once more, remaining regret to say, unfulfilled. Perhaps the Government may see fit to employ them later on. Meanwhile, I think it right to point out that a considerable number of the "pre-historics", who are only suffering from "anno domini", are strong, able bodied men, quite capable of bearing arms, and of shooting straight if necessary.'

For the first time ever Great Britain would have to bring in conscription, just over a year later, to ensure that it had enough men to carry on fighting the war against Germany and her allies. For some men the idea of enlisting in the armed forces and fighting in a war, was not something that they felt obliged to do. Not because they were cowards or conscientious objectors, but because they could not in all good conscience fight for a country whose politicians wanted to send them off to war, whilst at the same time refusing many of them the right to vote.

***SS** Anglia*

The steamship SS *Anglia* was owned by the London and North Western Railway Company, from whom it was requisitioned soon after the outbreak of the war. In April 1915 it was turned into a hospital ship, to ferry troops back to England who had been wounded on the battlefields of the Western Front. On 17 November 1915 she was making her way to Dover having left Calais with 390 wounded officers and men on board, when she struck a mine approximately one mile off shore and sank just east of Folkestone, making her the first hospital ship of the war to be sunk whilst carrying wounded personnel. There was a crew of twenty-eight as well as three Army doctors, three nurses and twenty-eight orderlies from the Royal Army Medical Corps (RAMC).

This was the same vessel on which King George V had sailed home after injuring himself on an earlier visit to the troops on the Western Front. Sadly eighty-five of those on board lost their lives, and most of them came from the front two wards, which could not be reached because of the damage caused by the initial explosion. Many of the wounded men were amputees and were therefore totally dependent on the nurses and orderlies of the RAMC who were caring for them.

HMS *Hazard*, one of the ships that was nearby at the time, came to the rescue. So did the collier *Lusitania* but whilst she was lowering her boats to pick up survivors, she too struck a mine and foundered, but thankfully all of her crew were saved. An article covering the story appeared in the *New York Times* on 18 November 1915.

Men from the Mercantile Marine made up the *Anglia*'s crew. Their bodies were not recovered and their names are commemorated on the Tower Hill Memorial in London:

Evans, R., Fireman – aged 43, a married man from Holyhead in Wales.

Thomas, Owen, Stoker – a 55-year-old married man who lived at Holyhead.

Thomas, Richard, Deck Boy – 16 years old, lived in Holyhead.

Wallace, Alfred, Steward – served under the surname of Jones, aged 31 and a single man who lived in Holyhead.

Williams, George Edward, Chief Engineer – aged 57, a married man from Caernarvon.

Williams, Joseph, Third Engineer – aged 32 and a single man from Holyhead.

Williams, Meredith, 2nd Steward – aged 28 and a single man from Holyhead.

Williams, Robert, Cabin Boy – aged 20 and a single man from Holyhead.

Lewis, John, Fireman – aged 41 and a married man from Holyhead.

Lewis, William, Quartermaster – aged 56 and a married man from Holyhead.

Owen, Thomas H., Galley Boy.

Parry, Thomas Richard, Seaman – aged 25 years and a single man from Caernarvon.

Pritchard, Robert, Trimmer – aged 20 and a single man from Holyhead.

Hughes, J, Cook – aged 28 and a single man from Holyhead.

Hughes, Lewis David, Engineer's Boy – a single man from Holyhead

Jones, Alfred, Steward – his surname was actually Wallace. He was 31 and a married man from Holyhead.

Jones, John, Fireman – aged 60 years and a married man from Holyhead.

Jones, Owen, Fireman – aged 45 and a married man from Holyhead.

Jones, Owen, Fireman – aged 28 and a married man from Gorton in Manchester.

Ashton, Albert Frederick, Cabin Boy – aged 19 and a single man from Holyhead.

Bassett, William Edward, Seaman – aged 50 and a married man from Holyhead.

Callaway, William Henry, Steward – aged 23 and a single man from Holyhead.

Campbell, N.J., Purser – aged 37 and a married man from Holyhead.

Redmond, James, Fireman – aged 29, born in Liverpool.

Stuart, R, Fireman.

The following men were orderlies with the Royal Army Medical Corps, whose job it was to care for the wounded men on board the *Anglia*:

Billot, Stanley, Private 8880, aged 36 .

Daltrey, Harry, Corporal 4998.

Doran, Edward Clement, Private 57953.

Hardy, Frank Albert, Private 7647. He was 19 and a single man from Bermondsey in London.

Heaton, Thomas, Private 11218, 12th Casualty Clearing Station, RAMC. He was 21 and a single man from Accrington in Lancashire.

Hodgkins, Ernest Victor Gardner, Private 18703. He was 31 and a married man from London.

Mortimer, Edward George Victor, Private 4996.

Rumble, Hubert William, Private 6395.

Worster, Walter Ernest, Private 1738, Royal Army Medical Corps. He was 26 and a single man from London.

The following are the wounded soldiers who were patients on board the *Anglia* and who died when she was sunk. Their names are commemorated on the Hollybrook Memorial at Southampton.

Allen, Robert Henry, Private 76124, 29th Battalion, Canadian Infantry. He was 30 and a single man from Westleigh in Lancashire.

Allen, William Andrew, Corporal 14010, 8th Battalion, South Lancashire Regiment.

Armstrong, William, Private S/8918, 8th Battalion, Seaforth Highlanders. He was 21 and a single man from Workington in Cumberland.

Ashley, Charles Willis, Private 4669, 8th Battalion, Lincolnshire Regiment. He was 18 and a single man from Scunthorpe in Lincolnshire.

Baker, Charles, Driver T1/2411, HQ, 14th Divisional Training Company, Army Service Corps. He was 24 and a single man.

Baldwin, John Jackson, Sergeant G/12, 7th Battalion, Royal Sussex Regiment. He was 27 and a single man from Walton-on-Thames.

Barber, Albert, Private 8660, 2nd Battalion, Suffolk Regiment. He had previously served as Private 10142 with the Bedfordshire Regiment. He was 21 and a single man from Bury-St-Edmunds in Suffolk.

Barlas, John, Private 22721, 11th (Service) Battalion Royal Scots (Lothian Regiment). He was 18 and a single man from Blairgowrie, Perthshire.

Bell, Christopher William, Private 13724, 10th Battalion, Yorkshire Regiment.

Biddlestone, Richard, Private 14415, 8th Battalion, East Yorkshire Regiment. He was 21 and a single man from Wolverhampton.

Biggins, James, Lance Corporal 18223, 12th Battalion, Sherwood Foresters (Nottinghamshire & Derbyshire Regiment).

Bird, William, Private 19768, 1st Battalion, Grenadier Guards.

Bishop, Lawrence Irvin, Private 11055, 2nd Battalion, Royal Scots.

Black, Robert, Private 413009, 26th Battalion, Canadian Infantry.

Bolding, Alfred William, Private 1464, 13th (Kensington) Battalion, London Regiment.

Bradbury, William, Private 21959, 2nd Battalion, Sherwood Foresters (Nottinghamshire & Derbyshire Regiment). He was 30 and a married man from Derby.

Bruce, William, Sapper 79663, 173rd Tunnelling Company, Royal Engineers, formerly Private 4693, Royal Scots.

Bycroft, William, Private 14379, 8th Battalion, Yorkshire Regiment. He was 20 and a single man from Middlesbrough.

Campbell, Arthur, Private 18106, 12th Battalion, Highland Light Infantry. He was 35 and a married man from Glasgow.

Palmer, William R., Private A/14404 (Served under the of surname Cann), 13th Battalion, (Quebec Regiment) Canadian Infantry.

Capps, Alfred Hanley, Private TF/2511, 1st/7th Battalion, Middlesex Regiment. He was 26 and a single man from London.

Carey, Patrick, Gunner 19790, 20th Siege Battery, Royal Garrison Artillery. He was 35 and a married man from Cork in Ireland.

Chapman, Albert James, Gunner 25633, 21st Trench Mortar Battery, Royal Field Artillery. He was 33 and a single man from Norwich.

Chorlton, Owen, Private 4963, 10th Battalion, (Prince of Wales's Own Royal) Hussars.

Clarkson, George, Private 17238, 1st Battalion, West Yorkshire (Prince of Wales's Own Royal) Hussars. He was 19 and a single man from Wortley in Leeds.

Coleman, John, Private 55803, 19th Battalion (Central Ontario), Canadian Infantry. He was 23 and a single man from Hamilton in Ontario, Canada.

Collins, John, Pioneer 120181, 8th Labour Battalion, Royal Engineers. He was 54 and a married man from Pontefract.

Colwell, Frederick, Private 18616, 9th Battalion, Devonshire Regiment. He was 17 and a single man from West Kensington, London.

Cox, John Herbert, Sapper 45, 4th Field Company, Canadian Engineers. He was 37 and a married man from Watford in Hertfordshire.

Curson, George, Private 7620, 2nd Battalion, Canadian Infantry.

Davies, Charles, Sergeant G/4594, 4th Battalion, Royal Fusiliers (City of London) Regiment.

Dobson, Stanley, Private 3164, 1st/5th Battalion, North Staffordshire Regiment.

Drewitt, William, Private 16674, 2nd Battalion, Royal Berkshire Regiment. He was 24 and a single man from Hungerford, Berkshire.

Drewery, Cornelius, Private 6500, Army Cyclist Corps. He had previously served as Private 13818, Wiltshire Regiment.

Duncan, Robert, Gunner 12899, 6th Division Ammunition Column, Royal Field Artillery.

Dunlop, James, Private S/8243, 9th Battalion, Seaforth Highlanders. He was 29 years and a married man from Glasgow.

Dymond, William Henry, Gunner 72164, 81st Brigade, Royal Field Artillery.

Eades, Joseph, Private 18836, 9th Battalion, South Staffordshire Regiment. He was 18 and a single man from Tipton in Staffordshire.

Eastwick, Harry, Private MS/1520, 18th Anti-Aircraft Section, Army Service Corps. He was 22 and a single man from Cheadle in Cheshire.

Eborall, Wilfred, Private 10617, 2nd Battalion, Wiltshire Regiment.

Ellis, Edward, Rifleman S/10169, 3rd Battalion, The Rifle Brigade. He was 32 and a married man from London.

Evans, Walter, Private 2160, 1st/5th Battalion, King's Own Yorkshire Light Infantry.

Fletcher, Henry, Lance Corporal 20126, 4th Battalion, Grenadier Guards. He was 32 and a married man from Royton, Oldham.

Frame, Robert, Gunner/Shoe Smith 903, III West Lancashire Brigade, Royal Field Artillery. He was 33 and a married man from Widnes, Lancashire.

Frankland, Arthur, Private 13079, 11th Battalion, (Prince of Wales's Own) West Yorkshire Regiment.

Fullwood, Emmanuel, Private 13931, 12th Battalion, Royal Scots. He was 18 and a single man from Glasgow.

Garrett, John, Private 24600, 13th Battalion (Royal Highlanders of Canada), Canadian Infantry.

Geddes, Percy Mannering, Private 9642, 3rd Battalion (Toronto Regiment), Canadian Infantry. He was 32 and a single man. He had previously served in the 2nd Boer War (1899-1902).

Gilday, John Michael, Lance Corporal 7688, 3rd Battalion, Coldstream Guards. He was 25 and a single man from Sheffield.

Gines, William Henry, Private 18747, 10th Battalion, Worcestershire Regiment. He was 19 and a single man from Knightwick in Worcester.

Goodwin, Thomas, Private 3978, 10th Battalion, Lancashire Fusiliers. He was 30 and a married man from Manchester.

Gower, Francis, Private SS/8728, 10th Labour Company, Army Service Corps.

Griffiths, John, Private 26315, B Company, 12th Battalion, Royal Scots. He was 17 and a single man form Manchester.

Griffiths, Tom, Gunner 96686, 38th Brigade Ammunition Column, Royal Field Artillery. He was 33 and a married man from Chesterfield.

Hales, Henry, Sapper 22340, Second Army HQ Signal Company, Royal Engineers.

Harris, Henry Thomas James, Sergeant TF/2142, 1st/8th Battalion, Middlesex Regiment.

Holmes, Ernest, Lance Corporal 17270, 6th Battalion, King's Own Scottish Borderers. He was 29 and a single man.

Hurwitz, Mark, Private 2999, 1st/7th Battalion, Sherwood Foresters (Nottinghamshire & Derbyshire Regiment).

Ingham, E., Private M209947, Army Service Corps.

Janin, George Alex Francis Romain, Major, HQ 2nd Division, Canadian Engineers.

Joly, Leonidas, Private 61477, 22nd Battalion (French Canadian), Canadian Infantry. He was 24 and a married man from Quebec, Canada.

Jones, Ellis, Sapper 102165, 175th Tunnelling Company, Royal Engineers.

Knight, George Ebenezer, Private 53350, 18th Battalion (Western Ontarion), Canadian Infantry.

Leathers, Cyril Robert, Sergeant 15077, 9th Battalion, Norfolk Regiment.

Leggett, John Rupert, Private 69510, 26th Battalion (New Brunswick), Canadian Infantry. He was 18 and a single man Boston in America.

McCormack, John, Private 16628, 7th Battalion, King's Own

Scottish Borderers. He was 36 and a married man from Greenock in Scotland.

McDonald, Archie, Lance Corporal 18221, 1st Battalion (Western Ontario), Canadian Infantry. He was 27 and a married man.

McEachern, Archibald Ernest, Private 227, Canadian Motor Machine Gun Brigade. He was 28 and a single man from, Ontario in Canada.

Mackay, James, Corporal 19817, 11th Battalion, Highland Light Infantry.

MacKenzie, John, Private 67548, 25th Battalion (Nova Scotia Rifles), Canadian Infantry. He was aged 25.

Mann, John, Private 312652, 2nd Battalion, York & Lancaster Regiment.

Marsh, William Charles, Corporal T/19969, 4th Company, 3rd Division Training Section, Army Service Corps. He was 27 and a married man from St Albans in Hertfordshire.

Miller, John, Private 22678, 12th Battalion, Royal Scots.

Miller, Richard, Corporal 10869, 10th Battalion, Prince of Wales's Own (West Yorkshire Regiment). He was 26 and a married man from Newcastle-on-Tyne.

Milton, Arthur, Private 74018, 28th Battalion (North-west), Canadian Infantry. He was 27 and a single man from Chertsey in Surrey.

Mooney, William, Private 680, Northumberland Hussars.

Moore, John, Private 12674, 10th Battalion, Lancashire Fusiliers.

Morrison, Robert, Private 12204, 9th Battalion, Duke of Wellington's (West Riding Regiment).

Moss, Herbert James, Gunner 780, 4th West Riding Brigade, Royal Field Artillery.

Myers, Kenneth, Gunner 33307, A Battery, 52nd Brigade, Royal Field Artillery. He was 19 and a single man from Sheffield.

Myson, Ernest, Sergeant 3/8400, 8th Battalion, Bedfordshire Regiment.

Napier, Henry Lenox, Major, 11th Battalion, Sherwood Foresters (Nottinghamshire & Derbyshire Regiment).

Nicholson, Henry James, Driver 5724, 1st Division, Signal Company, Royal Engineers. He was 28 and a married man from Montreal, Canada.

Orton, Elias, Private 22139, 2nd Battalion, Sherwood Foresters (Nottinghamshire & Derbyshire Regiment). He was 27 and a married man from Doncaster in Yorkshire.

Pain, George William, Driver 2877, 7th Field Company, Royal Field Artillery.

Parden, Frank, Private 23255, 12th Battalion, The King's (Liverpool Regiment).

Pearson, James, Private 22208, 2nd Battalion, Durham Light Infantry. He was 34 and a married man from Hartlepool.

Pearson, Robert William, Private M2/076062, GHQ, Troops Supply Column, Army Service Corps.

Perry, George Montague, Private 56140, 19th Battalion (Central Ontario), Canadian Infantry.

Ponton, Maitland Archibald, Private 66128, 24th Battalion, Canadian Infantry. He was 25 and a single man.

Priestley, Trueman, Private 533840, 18th Battalion (Western Ontario), Canadian Infantry.

Pyper, David, Private 430187, 31st Battalion (Alberta), Canadian Infantry. He was a married man from Manitoba in Canada.

Ridichan, Patrick, Private 24477, 10th Battalion, Highland Light Infantry.

Robinson, Harry, Private 3807, 1st/6th Battalion, Prince of Wales's Own (West Yorkshire Regiment).

Ryan, Michael, Private 4482, 2nd Battalion, Leinster Regiment. Formerly Private 100270, Royal Field Artillery.

Shelley, John Archibald, Driver 1194, 1st/4th Battalion West Lancashire Brigade, Royal Field Artillery.

Shepherd, George, Rifleman 2077, 1st/7th Battalion, Prince of Wales's Own (West Yorkshire Regiment).

Simpson, Charles William, Private 1341, Army Cyclist Corps. Formerly Rifleman 1785, Rifle Brigade.

Smith, Arthur J., Corporal 10529, 2nd Battalion, Highland Light Infantry. He was 27 and a single man from London.

Smith, Harry, Private L/6303, 1st Battalion, The Buffs (East Kent Regiment).

Smith, James, Private 12175, 9th Battalion, Cameronians (Scottish Rifles).

Southam, William George, Private 12024, 6th Battalion, Dorsetshire Regiment. He was 34 and a single man from Stratford-on-Avon.

Steers, W.A., Private 438555, 3rd Battalion, Canadian Infantry. He was 36 and a married man who lived in Ivybridge in Devon.

Sullivan, Samuel, Driver 28631, 3rd Division Ammunition Column, Royal Field Artillery.

Taylor, Charles Harry, Lieutenant, 10th Battalion, Prince of Wales's Own (West Yorkshire Regiment). He was 29 and a single man who lived in Wolverhampton.

Taylor, James, Private G/7272, 1st Battalion, Middlesex Regiment.

Tharratt, George Vanes, Lieutenant, 4th Battalion, The King's (Liverpool Regiment). He was 20 and a single man from Liverpool.

Turpin, Richard Dawson, Corporal 9926, 10th Battalion, York and Lancaster Regiment.

Turton, Frederick, Private 2690, 1st /15th Battalion, King's Own Yorkshire Light Infantry.

Twist, William Edward, Lance Corporal 8688, 10th Battalion Yorkshire Regiment. He was 32 and a married man from Thornaby-on-Tees in County Durham.

White, Henry Richard, Corporal 9620, 2nd Battalion, Royal Berkshire Regiment.

White, William, Private 11874, 7th Battalion, East Yorkshire Regiment. He was 20 years of age and a single man from Firth Park, Sheffield.

Williams, John, Private 2009, 7th Battalion, The King's (Liverpool Regiment).

Williams, Robert, Rifleman S/4050, 13th Battalion, Rifle Brigade. He was 26 and a single man from the Ship and Castle Hotel in Caernarvon.

Wood, Joshua, Private 2519, 1st/6th Battalion, Prince of Wales's Own (West Yorkshire Regiment). He was 18 and a single man from Mansfield, Nottingham.

Wright, John Thomas, Private 5675, 5th Battalion, Royal Irish Lancers. He was 19 and a single man from Birmingham.

Wynne, James, Private 4056, 2nd Battalion, Sherwood Foresters (Nottinghamshire & Derbyshire Regiment).

Youngs, Arthur Ernest, 15698, 9th Battalion, Norfolk Regiment. He was 21 and a single man from Coltishall. Norwich.

Searching the internet for information on the sinking of HMHS *Anglia* there are different figures bandied about concerning the actual numbers of men and women who died on that fateful day. The Commonwealth War Graves Commission website records that a total of 152 men and women lost their lives when the *Anglia* was sunk on 17 November 1915. This included Staff Nurse, Mary Rodwell from the Queen Alexandra's Imperial Military Nursing Corps; twenty-five members of the *Anglia*'s crew, most of whom lived in Holyhead in Wales; nine members of the RAMC, who served as orderlies and 117 wounded and sick officers and men from numerous regiments, who were from all over the British Isles and Canada. None of these men, or Staff Nurse Rodwell, ever had their bodies recovered, but along with the survivors, nine bodies were brought into Dover Harbour on the afternoon of 17 November.

The sinking of the *Anglia* showed just how many communities could be affected by just one incident. The ship was due to arrive at Dover where the loss would have been particularly felt. All of the regiments in which the men were serving would have been deeply saddened at their loss, especially in the circumstances in which they died. The community of Holyhead, where most of the crew were from, grieved for their collective loss, whilst the individual families had to deal with the pain of the physical loss of a loved one.

A man being wounded in battle was bad enough, especially when it resulted in an amputation, but after reaching the sanctuary of a hospital ship to have lives snatched away in such tragic circumstances, seems so unfair – but then nobody ever said that war was fair.

The following article appeared in the *Dover Express* on Friday, 19 November 1915:

HOSPITAL SHIP SUNK

'The War Office reports that the hospital ship "Anglia" struck a mine in the Channel today and sank. The total number on board was 13 officers and 372 other ranks, of whom about 300 were saved by a patrol vessel.

Another vessel proceeding to the rescue was also sunk by another mine.

The names of those who lost their lives will be communicated to their next of kin and made public without delay.

The First Lord of the Admiralty has received from Lord Stamfordham on behalf of the King, the following message:-

"His Majesty is grieved at the loss incurred, and trusts that survivors have not unduly suffered from the terrible exposure to which they must have been subjected. Please express the King's heartfelt sympathy with the families of those who have perished."'

The news of the sinking reached Dover a few hours after it had taken place, creating an atmosphere of shock and disbelief after initial reports had suggested that all of those who had been bed ridden, some 200 people in total, had perished. The survivors started arriving at Dover Harbour early in the afternoon, brought there by several vessels who had gone to the *Anglia*'s assistance. Some of those who were brought ashore were already dead and they, along with others who were in a serious condition, were conveyed to the town's military hospital.

The mine which the *Anglia* had struck had been laid by the German submarine UC-5. The manner in which the submarine had laid the mines, which clearly put in danger non-military vessels from neutral countries not engaged in warfare, was therefore in breach of the Hague Convention.

UC-5 was responsible for sinking twenty-nine Allied ships during the war. Her war ended on 27 April 1916 when she ran aground while

UC-5 On display in Central Park in New York City

on patrol. Her crew then attempted to scuttle her but the explosives failed to go off. All of the crew were captured by HMS *Firedrake* and UC-5 was recovered undamaged and subsequently put on display in London on the River Thames, and in Central Park in New York City.

CHAPTER FOUR

1916 – The Realization

With the war now into its third year there was a realization, both on a political level as well as amongst the general population, that the war was not going to be over any time soon. By the beginning of 1916, British and Dominion military casualties had already reached a staggering 189,384, which equates to approximately 370 lives lost for each day. By the end of 1916 a further 237,351 British and Dominion men had been killed, which meant that the daily average figure for the number of men killed had risen to approximately 485.

The cost in financial terms was unbelievable. By the end of the war Great Britain alone had spent an estimated £3.5 billion. This equated to £761,904,762 each month, meaning that for every day of the war, the cost to Great Britain was approximately £25 million. What makes these financial figurers even more staggering is that they represent the actual cost, not an equivalent cost in today's money.

The war in a political sense had become somewhat of a catch twenty-two situation, as the cost in both human life and financial burden had already reached crippling proportions, with still no obvious end to the conflict in sight. It was questionable how much longer Britain could manage to sustain such a financial commitment whilst incurring casualties at the rate they had up until that time. The alternative view was that regardless of the financial cost and the continued loss of life, Britain and her Allies had simply gone too far to stop now.

The year 1916 would be recorded in the annals of history as being a bloody and brutal time. The longest battle of the war took place in 1916: the Battle of Verdun, which lasted from 21 February to 18

December and resulted in an estimated 337,000 casualties for both France and Germany.

Something which had far reaching ramifications for most men in Great Britain in 1916 was conscription which came into force on 27 January 1916. All British men who as of 15 August 1915 had been living in this country and were aged between 19 and 41 were subject to the conditions of the Military Service Act. The Act also included all males who as of 2 November 1915 were unmarried or a widowed without any dependant children.

As with every rule, there were always exemptions, the Military Service Act was no different. Those who were exempt included men who were in the following categories:

- men who were resident in the Dominions or who were only resident in Great Britain for their education or some other special purpose

- men who were already serving in the Reserve Forces or the Territorial Army, who were either liable for foreign service, or who were, in the opinion of the Army Council, not suitable for foreign service

- men who were already serving in the Royal Navy or the Royal Marines; men who were regular ministers of any religious faith

- men who had previously served with the military or Navy and been discharged on grounds of ill-health or the termination of their service

- men who held a certificate of exemption from having to undertake military service or who had tried to enlist since 4 August 1914 and were rejected.

A man could make an application to be classified as being exempt from having to undergo military service, on four grounds. These were: that it was in the national interest for him to be engaged in other work, or because he was being educated or trained in that work and that it should continue; that serious financial hardship would befall a man and his family owing to his exceptional financial or business obligations should he be called upon to enlist, and anyone who was in ill health or infirmity.

The final exemption was somewhat unique. As this was the first time that Britain had ever had to conscript men to join the armed forces, it was written in to the Act that men were allowed to refuse to undertake combatant service, on the grounds of conscientious objection.

Interestingly government departments could issue certificates of exemption to men or groups of men in their employ, where it was deemed to be more convenient to do so, rather than have these men make individual applications through Local Tribunals. Certificates of Exemption could be temporary, with conditions, or absolute, but the onus was on the individual to inform the authorities if the conditions as to why the certificate of exemption had been granted, changed. Failure to do so could result in a maximum sentence of six months imprisonment with hard labour.

Each district of the country as defined by the National Registration Act 1915, had a Local Tribunal in place to deal with these cases. Part of the process included a system which allowed for individuals to appeal the decision of a tribunal, which could be made up of between five and twenty-five members.

Any individual who had been issued with an official War Service Badge by the War Office before 1 March 1916, due to working for either the Admiralty of the Ministry of Munitions, was counted as though they were in possession of a certificate of exemption.

On 25 February 1916 a Local Tribunal took place in the Mayor's chambers at the Town Hall in Dover. There were seven members of the panel including the Mayor, Mr Farley, and two military representatives, Dr Pinhorn and Mr E. Bradley.

The meeting commenced with one of the members, Mr W. Robson complaining about unsolicited correspondence he and other members of the tribunal had received from an unknown individual which he felt was attempting to unduly influence the decisions he made as a member of the Dover Tribunal. Mr Robson was understandably perplexed and angry about the conduct of this particular individual and commented

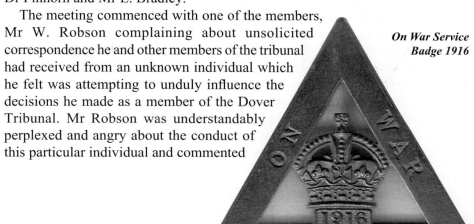

On War Service Badge 1916

that he felt whoever was responsible for circulating the literature was also committing an offence under the Defence of the Realm Act.

Mr Vosper, the clerk to the Tribunal, said that he felt that it was not only an improper thing to do but very risky also. The Mayor stated that he did not believe that the literature in question would have any effect on how they voted, individually or collectively, and would therefore have no effect on the eventual outcome of any of the appeals which would appear before them.

Dr Pinhorn, one of the two military representatives, posed the question as to whether or not an applicant, who was appearing before the committee, had the right to determine if their individual case should not be heard in public. Mr Vosper clarified the situation by explaining that under the Military Service Act, which the appeals were governed by, all such hearings should be held in public unless the Tribunal acceded to a request made by a claimant for all or any part of the proceedings to be heard in private.

Because of the stigma attached to those who did not want to enlist in His Majesty's armed forces, many people did not necessarily want the circumstances of their particular case spread all over the pages of the press.

The first of the claims for exemption that the Tribunal committee dealt with on 25 February, concerned Mr Frank Tritton who lived at the River Post Office. He tended to dairy cows and chickens and claimed that the business could not be run solely by his brother, whose main work was that of a baker, and his mother and sisters were occupied full time with the Post Office. He informed the Tribunal that if he was forced to enlist, his mother would have to dispose of the cows.

Mr Tritton was given a two month exemption, at which time he would have to re-appear before the Tribunal, and re-appeal his case if he saw fit to do so. In lots of cases when they handed out such short exemptions to the applicant, they were in essence providing him with sufficient time to put their personal affairs in order.

The 1911 Census showed the Tritton family did in fact live at the Post Office, River, Dover. Head of the family was widow Amelia Triton aged 63. Her occupation was shown as being a baker as well as the Sub Post Mistress. Her eldest daughter, Ellen, was an assistant in the Post Office, and Bertha was a book keeper, also in the Post Office.

Her younger son, George, was shown as being an accountant's clerk, but there was no mention of his also being a baker. As for Frank, he was shown as being a carpenter and joiner, but there was no mention of any dairy cows or chickens. It is of course more than possible that in the five years between 1911 and 1916, George and Frank both changed their occupations.

The next case before the Tribunal was that of Arthur Giscard Treleaven, a chef and confectioner who worked at a café in Folkestone owned by Mr W. Hollis. It was in fact Mr Hollis who was making the application on behalf of Mr Treleaven, on the grounds that the man's services were necessary for the kitchen to properly operate. There were eleven other people employed in the café, and they could end up out of a job if he lost Mr Treleaven. Mr Hollis informed the Tribunal that since the war had started, seven members of his staff had left his employ to enlist in the Army. The outcome was somewhat of a pyrrhic victory for Mr Hollis as the Tribunal granted a three-month postponement, but only so that he could find an older chef to replace Mr Treleaven.

Arthur Giscard Treleaven was born in Kentish Town, London, in 1881, at the outbreak of the war he was 33 years of age and had been living with his parents, Richard and Julie Treleaven and his younger brother Francis, at 41 Belgrave Road, Leyton, in London. Francis, who was a clerk by way of occupation, enlisted in the Army Service Corps in London on 8 December 1915 and was then placed on the Army Reserve. He was mobilized on 14 October 1916, and on 29 November 1917, he was discharged as no longer physically fit for war service, as per King's Regulations, Paragraph 392 (xvi). There was no detailed explanation on his service record of the reasons for this. A condition of his discharge was that he was liable to be sent a statutory order on 29 November 1918 requiring him to present himself for medical re-examination under the Military Service Review of Exceptions Act 1917. In view of the Armistice, I doubt very much if the order was ever sent out to him.

Mr Stanley Edward Tilbrook proved to be an interesting case. Why he came before the Dover Military Tribunal is not absolutely clear, as he was a native of Ipswich in Suffolk and worked in London. To be precise he was a cook at the Burlington Hotel, Cork Street in London, and applied for an exemption on the grounds of ill health, but was unable to attend the Tribunal hearing owing to ill health, which still went ahead in his absence.

Mr Vosper pointed out to his colleagues that Mr Tilbrook was an attested man and that a Tribunal was in place to deal with unattested men who were trying to claim an exemption. Dr Pinhorn stated that as Mr Tilbrook had already attested, he needed to be re-examined by the Army doctor. Mr Tilbrook was accordingly informed in writing of the Tribunal's decision.

Walter Samuel West, a greengrocer of 5 Lorne Road, Dover, applied for an exemption on the grounds that he was the sole support of a widowed mother and that she was in poor health after having had a 'break down' some six months earlier. Mr West stated that he paid his weekly takings as a greengrocer, which was on average thirty shillings a week to his mother for food and board. The case was adjourned for a month so that enquiries could be made to ascertain whether Mrs West would be financially better off if she was in receipt of a soldier's dependant's allowance.

This was somewhat of a strange affair as Walter, who was born in 1884 at Ramsgate, had attested on 4 February 1916 at Dover, and became Private 29219 West of the Suffolk Regiment, some three weeks before his Tribunal date. It can only be assumed that the members of the Tribunal were not aware that he had already enlisted, and that Walter didn't tell them. As Tribunals were for unattested men, why Walter was appealing against having to enlist isn't clear.

Walter was 32 years of age when he enlisted, but only weighed 7 stones 10 pounds, and at only 5ft 1in tall with a 29in chest, he most definitely wasn't the biggest of men. He was mobilized on 12 May 1916 and was posted to B Company, 10th Battalion, Suffolk Regiment at Bury St Edmunds, but it must have quickly become apparent to Walter's instructors that he was not going to be able to deal with the rigours of military service, because just seventy-three days later, on 22 July, he was discharged for not likely to become an efficient soldier.

Maybe the pressure on recruiting centres, coupled with the financial incentives to sign men up, was the reason why Walter was deemed to be 'fit for service in the field at home and abroad', when he was medically examined at Dover on 4 February 1916, by Lieutenant Piery of the Royal Army Medical Corps. Form B. 204 had to be completed by the Army if it was looking to have a recruit discharged on the grounds that they were not likely to become and efficient soldier. Under the heading of, 'Cause of objection to be fully stated', it read as follows: 'Mentally and physically weak. Cannot do drills or marching and cannot remember or understand orders.'

Walter's case highlights the pressure placed upon recruitment centres, by the Government, to sign up more and more men to fight in the war. With the greatest respect to Walter's memory, it must have been blatantly obvious from his physical appearance that he was never going to make it through his basic training, let alone be suited to the physical demands and rigours of being a soldier in wartime.

The year 1916 was also notable for the excesses of German submarines throughout the Mediterranean, English Channel and North Sea. In that one year alone, 415 Allied merchant ships were sunk by these assassins of the German Navy. The people of Dover had seen at first hand the devastating effect of such attacks with the sinking of the P&O passenger liner, the SS *Maloja*, just two nautical miles off the coast of Dover. Her regular route was between Tilbury in Essex and Bombay in India. She was a formidable vessel capable of a top speed of nineteen knots with a capacity to carry a maximum of 670 passengers as well as cargo.

The winter months from November 1915 until March 1916 were particularly severe, with high winds and heavy snowfalls, when the SS *Maloja* set sail from the Port of Tilbury on the Essex coast for Bombay on 26 February. On board that fateful day were Captain C.D. Irving, Royal Naval Reserve, with a crew of 301 officers and men, mainly made up of Lascars, a term used for sailors who originated from the Indian sub-continent. There were also 122 passengers on board, mostly Government and military personnel and their families.

The *Maloja* made her way slowly along the River Thames, before passing through the Straits of Dover and into the English Channel. Just off Dover disaster struck, although at first it wasn't known whether she had been torpedoed by a German submarine or had struck a mine. It later transpired that despite defensive measures by the Royal Navy to stop German vessels from passing through the English Channel, the

P&O Passenger Liner SS **Maloja**

German U-Boat Seiner Majestat (SM) UC-6, a mine laying submarine of the German Imperial Navy, had laid the offending mine.

Captain Irving, had taken the decision of sailing with his ship's lifeboats swung out over the water, as a precautionary measure. Having struck the mine, the *Maloja*'s engine room quickly started to flood, which prevented Captain Irving from bringing his ship to a complete standstill. This, coupled with the ship starting to list, also meant that having given the order to prepare to abandon ship, it was only possible to launch a few of the lifeboats.

The *Maloja* sank in under twenty-five minutes, but as she had been so close to shore when she struck the mine, it was possible for rescue ships to get to her relatively quickly, this included two of the Port of Dover's tug boats, *Lady Brassey* and *Lady Crundall*. Even so, 155 passengers and crew lost their lives, and only forty-five bodies were recovered.

Dover's St Mary the Virgin cemetery contains a monument to twenty-two of the Lascars who died when the *Maloja* was sunk. It also contains the graves of civilians, including women and children who also lost their lives. There are also three members of the Mercantile Marine buried there, along with two from the Army and one from the Navy. They were:

Bed Steward Alfred William Lucas
Bed Steward John Fitch Kemp

Stewardess E. Maberley
Second Lieutenant Indian Army Reserve Officer Henry James
Fraser
Senior Assistant Surgeon, Lieutenant W.J.S. Maine, Indian
Subordinate Medical Department
Chief Shipwright (175985) Samuel Colwill, Royal Navy. His
widow, Ann Colwill, lived in Plymouth.

On 29 February a sixty-strong contingent of the Dover Co-operative
Junior Choir visited the Oil Mill Barracks and provided a concert to
200 men of the Royal East Surrey Regiment, who thoroughly enjoyed
the evening's entertainment. Besides the choir, there was a fine solo
display on the piano, by Miss Doris Cook, and an equally good singing
performance provided by Miss Doris Winter, who was forced to return
to the stage for an encore, at which time she gave a rendition of 'Two
blue Eyes', and provided much amusement when she sang the song,
'I do like a s'nice s'mince pie'. Another singer, Mary O'Flaherty was
also requested by an appreciative audience, to return and sing further
songs, which she did in the form of 'Annie Laurie' and 'If all the
hearts'. There were also vocal offerings provided by Masters Montie
de Orfe and Eddie Vine, as well as Vena Bromley, Nellie Fleet and
Olive Cook.

   The choir brought the evening to an end by singing two humorous
songs, which were cheered by the men of the Royal East Surrey
Regiment, who applauded heartedly and gave three cheers at the end of
the performance as a means of showing their thanks and appreciation
for the evening's entertainment.

   On 31 March at Dover Police Court, Mr Raymond Cook, of 2
Hortus Villa, Barton Road, Dover, was before magistrates, Mr F.G.
Wright and Dr C. Wood, on a charge of writing a postcard containing
information which might be useful to the enemy. Mr Cook pleaded
guilty to the charge, but stated that he was innocent of any wrong
doing or intent.

   Mr Vosper, from the Town Clerk's office, said that the case had been
determined worthy of prosecution to emphasize the need for members
of the public to be careful and diligent in their private correspondence.
This was a subject that had been highlighted across the district since

the beginning of the war, both in the local newspaper and by means of posters.

Raymond Cook sent a postcard to his aunt who lived in Newcastle, in which he gave his version of an air raid which took place on Dover on 19 March. His account of what took place was, in some respects, very misleading. Mr Vosper, the Clerk of the Court, made the somewhat strange observation that he thought writing such a communication was wrong and that he could not understand why Mr Cook had done what he had.

Mr Cook replied that his only intention was to let his aunt know that he was safe and well.

Mr Vosper pointed out that he could have done that without saying what he did. Mr Cook apologised for his actions, but added that he expected a good many other people had done the same.

The magistrates fined Mr Cook £1 and hoped that the case would be a lesson to others, and that it would stop them from committing the same offence.

An Old Dovorian Roll of Honour, which contained the names and details of all the past members of Dover College who had served their king and country had been compiled by Mrs F.R.G. Duckworth, who was the daughter of a former headmaster of the college, and Captain C.L. Evans, who was the commanding officer of the Dover College Officers' Training Corps. The roll contained 652 names. The following bravery awards had been handed out to some of the men named on the Roll of Honour: one CB, five CMGs, twelve DSOs, thirteen MCs, one DCM, five Croix de Chevaliers; forty-seven were Mentioned in Despatches. Sixty-five had been killed, fifty-nine had been wounded and seven had been reported missing or had been taken prisoner.

A vellum-bound copy of the Roll of Honour was submitted to the King by Lord Northbourne, in his capacity as the chairman of the college's governing body. The King in return expressed the opinion that the College had every reason to be proud of the record of the war services of its former boys, and felt as patron, that everyone who had an interest in Dover College must have been grateful for the care and trouble bestowed on the compilation of the Roll of Honour.

At the beginning of April 1916 an inquest was held at the Western

Heights Military Hospital, by the Borough Coroner, Mr Sydenham Payn, on the body of Joseph Luige, who was 37 years of age.

In evidence Lieutenant M.A. Simson said:

'The body viewed at the mortuary is that of Joseph Luige, in the East Surrey Regiment, aged 37 years. He lived at 18 Old Town, Croydon. On Saturday evening at about 7 o'clock, I was crossing the barracks when I heard a thud, and saw a man lying about twenty yards from me on the ground, near the balcony which is boarded in. I went to him and turned him over and he was bleeding from the right side of the jaw and the right ear. I called for help, and he was placed on a stretcher and brought to the hospital. He was unconscious. I found his name written on his trousers. He attested on 30th March, and was in the Army one day.'

Private R.H. Toras said in evidence:

'I was on the balcony in question at 7pm, and saw a man rush out of the last door on the landing. He put one foot on the bottom rail and he gave a spring and fell over the wooden boarding. He did not make a murmur. I was some distance off. I went indoors and gave the alarm. It frightened me, and I could not go near him. I saw him removed. I do not know him.'

The next to give his evidence was Private G.W. Martin:

'I have known the deceased for about five years. We joined together at Croydon. He was an organ grinder and an Italian. I used to turn the handle for him sometimes. We did not get much profit. Work was a bit slack, so the deceased joined the Army. He was well when we came down, but he did not seem very cheerful. On the first night we came here he complained of a pain in his stomach. When we got to bed he leaned against an iron bar and beckoned me to him, and I went and caught him as he fainted. I laid him on his bed, and he complained of pains in his stomach. He was taken away by the ambulance, and the next morning he said that he was all right. I saw him at breakfast time, about 8am. He did not come down for breakfast or dinner. I asked him on Saturday how he felt, and I received the same answer as on

Friday. I saw him in the afternoon, and we had a cup of tea. He
was a bit miserable when we left the canteen, and that was the
last I saw of him.'

The last person to give their evidence was Lieutenant A.J.L. Speechly,
of the Royal Army Medical Corps. He said:

'I saw the deceased on Saturday evening. He was unconscious
and suffering from fracture of the base of the skull, a fracture of
the lower jaw, and there was a cut about two inches long on the
chin. The cause of death was the fractured base of the skull. He
lived about two hours, but never regained consciousness. The fall
from the balcony caused the fracture.'

A verdict of suicide during temporary insanity was returned by the
jury. This was a sad case, where a man who had only been in the Army
for one day, found life so difficult, that not only did his best friend not
notice anything wrong with him, but that Joseph felt unable to share
his feelings with anybody else.

Two hugely significant battles which changed the course of the war
took place in 1916, the Battle of Jutland and the Battle of the Somme.

Jutland, which has gone down in history as the largest naval battle
with the greatest loss of life, took place in the North Sea off the west
coast of Denmark between 31 May and 1 June. It involved vessels from
the Royal Navy's Grand Fleet, under the command of Admiral Sir John
Jellicoe together with Vice Admiral Sir David Beatty commanding
the British Battlecruiser Fleet and 5th Battle Squadron. The Imperial
German High Seas Fleet was commanded by Vice-Admiral Reinhard
Scheer.

Jutland was claimed by both sides as a victory, which was somewhat
at odds with the number of ships and men which each side lost. The
British lost fourteen major ships, including HMS *Indefatigable*,
HMS *Invincible* and HMS *Queen Mary* whilst the Germans lost nine.
German losses were 507 officers and men wounded, with a further
2,551 killed. British casualties were 674 wounded, 6,094 killed, with
a further 177 who were captured and taken prisoner. The Royal Navy
was able to maintain its blockade of the German fleet which is seen as
an important factor in the Allies' eventual victory.

The Battle of the Somme, which has been described as 'hell on earth' took place between 1 July and 18 November. On the first day of the battle – the worst in the history of the British Army – Allied forces incurred approximately 57,000 casualties, 20,000 of whom were killed. This followed immediately after a week-long artillery barrage of German defensive lines, which continued non-stop and saw an estimated one million artillery shells being fired, not all of which detonated.

There have always been disagreements as to the actual numbers of casualties from all sides during the battle, mainly because both sides used different criteria to determine this information, but it is still universally accepted that in excess of one million men from all sides were either wounded or killed by the end of the battle. Interestingly, when checking on the Commonwealth War Graves Commission website for the same dates as the Battle of the Somme, their records show a total of 139,470 men who were killed and either buried or commemorated in France. It also records the actual British and Commonwealth losses for those killed on the first day of the battle, as being 18,543.

The Battle of Flers-Courcelette, which took place on 15 September, saw tanks used by the British for the first time in the war and, although not a total success, their effectiveness improved as the war went on.

November 28 saw the first German raid by an aircraft, rather than a Zeppelin, take place over the south coast of England. Gotha bombers were used during the raid, which in the main was focused on the City of London.

There was a change of British Prime Minister on 7 December when David Lloyd George replaced Herbert Asquith. To many this was far from a surprise and long overdue as Asquith appeared to have a 'wait and see' approach to the war. He seemed happier responding to circumstances as they unfolded rather than going on the attack and dictating the course and speed of the war, as Lloyd George wanted.

There was a feeling amongst many that the British Government under Asquith had been both slack and inefficient in their approach and attitude to the war. The end came when Lloyd George requested that a War Council be raised which was to consist of five members, excluding Asquith. On the evening of 4 December Asquith promised a reshuffle of the Ministry, but refused Lloyd George's demands. Lloyd George and other government members resigned which left

Asquith with no alternative but to take the same course of action. After a discussion, which including the King and other leading statesmen, Lloyd George was invited to form a government, which he accepted. For many observers this was a major turning point in the war.

The Cannon family at war

Henry and Emma Cannon lived at 7 Lower Hillside Road, Buckland in Dover, and it was certainly a tight squeeze in their household. Besides their nine sons, Emma's two children from her previous marriage, Annie and Fred Sayer, also lived with them.

Henry and Emma had married on 26 June 1886 in Dover. When Henry enlisted as a Pioneer (295683) in the Labour Corps, Royal Engineers, on 13 October 1915 in London, he was already 46 years of age. He was discharged from the Army on 5 December 1917 as being no longer physically fit for war service.

Incredibly six of Henry and Emma's sons also enlisted and fought during the war. Henry Thomas junior was Henry and Emma's eldest son. He was born on 2 April 1887 in Dover and joined the Royal

The crew of HMAS Australia December 1918

Navy on 3 March 1906 aged 18. He was a Stoker (SS102645), and the first and last ship that he served on, was HMS *Acheson*. After he had completed five years' service in the Navy, having served for the period he had signed up for, he was then placed on the Navy Reserve in 1911, before being re-called at the outbreak of the First World War. He kept the same rank as he had previously held and found himself as part of the crew of the battle cruiser HMAS *Australia*.

First commissioned on 21 June 1913 at Portsmouth, this was the Australian Navy's first flagship. She was scuttled off Sydney on 12 April 1924. Henry survived the war, and was demobbed on 2 July 1922.

Another son, Albert J. Cannon, was a stoker on board HMS *Diamond*.

Daniel Edward Thomas Cannon was born in Dover in 1895. He enlisted in the Royal Navy on 30 March 1911 at the age of 16, his first ship being HMS *Ganges*. He became an Ordinary Seaman on 24 October 1912 and an Able Seaman (J11807) on 26 November 1913. His last ship, HMS *Formidable*, was the one he was serving on when he was killed in action on 1 January 1915.

At the outbreak of war *Formidable*, which was one of the ships of the 5th Battle Squadron, was based at Portland in Dorset, but on 14 November 1914 the Squadron was moved to Sheerness in Kent because of the belief at that time that a German invasion of England was a real possibility. On New Year's Eve the Squadron, including the *Formidable*, was involved in gunnery exercises off the Isle of Portland. At 0220 hours on 1 January 1915 the *Formidable*, under the command of Captain Noel Loxley, was struck by a torpedo fired by the German submarine U-24 and within twenty minutes she was already listing badly. Forty-five minutes later she was hit by a second torpedo and soon after 0445 hours, she sank.

Out of a crew of 780 officers and men, 35 officers and 512 men, including 21-year-old Daniel Cannon, lost their lives with the sinking of the *Formidable*. Captain Loxley's fox terrier, Butch, which was with him on the bridge at the time of the sinking, also died. His body was washed up on the Dorset coastline.

The U-24 sank thirty-four Allied ships during the course of the war. She was surrendered to the British on 22 November 1918.

Daniel's body was not recovered and he is commemorated on the Chatham Naval Memorial.

George H. Cannon was born on 9 August 1896 and enlisted in the Navy at Chatham on 7 May 1912, when he was only 15 years old. On 9 August 1914, on his 18th birthday, he signed on to serve for a further 12 years as an Able Seaman (J/16907). Like his brother Daniel, the first ship that he served on was HMS *Ganges*. George survived the war and at the end of it, he remained in the Navy to complete the twelve years' service which he had signed up for, finally leaving the Navy on 4 March 1925. He had enlisted as a boy and left as a 28-year-old married man, having wed Kathleen Howlett in November 1917.

Unlike his four brothers, Harold Ross Cannon did not enlist in the Royal Navy, but instead joined the Army, the Royal Field Artillery. There were at least three men of that name who served with the Royal Field Artillery during the course of the First World War. Looking through the British Army's Medal Rolls Index cards for each of them, I was not able to distinguish between them, although one of them transferred to the Royal Engineers on 29 September 1916.

As 1916 drew to a close Germany had time to reflect on what was becoming an increasingly painful war, both in a human sense, as well as a financial one. She had spent ten months of the year fighting the French at the Battle of Verdun between 21 February and 18 December, during which time she had sustained almost 400,000 casualties, 143,000 of whom had been killed. At the same time Germany was also involved in the Battle of the Somme, which took place between 1 July and 18 November, where she sustained a further 500,000 casualties, some 200,000 of whom were killed.

With this as a background Germany attempted to negotiate a peace with Britain and her Allies. At this stage of the war, America was still a neutral nation and it was the US President, Woodrow Wilson, who offered to intervene and act as a peacemaker. Germany preferred to speak and deal directly with Britain. Lloyd George and his cabinet took a hard stance against the German offer of a negotiated peace. They sought financial restoration for the damage caused by the German war machine, but not just for herself but for all of her Allies as well. They wanted Germany to remove her armies from all of the lands which she had occupied during the war. The Entente powers of the Allied nations, would not even begin such peace negotiations until Germany had acquiesced to these demands. Germany refused, and so the war continued for two more bloody years at a cost of hundreds of thousands of lives.

CHAPTER FIVE

1917 – Seeing it through

Lloyd George and his government had taken a hard line in response to the German offer of a negotiated peace in December 1916. It can only be guessed what the British response would have been if Asquith and his supporters had still been in office. By the end of 1916 British and Dominion losses recorded by the CWGC were 237,377, which means that on average 650 men were killed every day of the year. The figures for those wounded in the same time span would, as an estimation, be around double the figure of those who were killed.

According to a recent paper published in *The Lancet* of those men who were wounded during the same time period, 41,000 of them were surviving amputees, which for the year 1917, would have been somewhere in the region of 9,000.

After Lloyd George had turned down Germany's offer of peace, all knew that 1917 was going to be a crucial year, as the Allies pushed on to win the war and secure a victory on their terms.

I will first take a look at general matters before taking in the year's major battles in more detail.

The first really big piece of news of the new year that was a potential game changer was Germany's announcement on 1 February that it was to resume its policy of unrestricted submarine warfare, which in effect meant that any Allied, or neutral shipping that was believed to be on its way to Great Britain, was seen as a legitimate target, as Germany attempted to win the war by blockading and starving the British of much needed foodstuffs and military hardware.

The very next day the British Government issued a voluntary

Women's Land Army Poster

rationing scheme, in an attempt to make the public consider how much food they consumed. The fear of running out of food was a real and present danger, because if it ever got to that stage the only sensible option left to the British Government was an unconditional surrender which was unthinkable.

February also saw the formation of the British organization for female civilians, the Women's Land Army. Its purpose was to fill the gaps left in farming and agriculture, by men being called up or volunteering for military service. The women were affectionately known as 'Land Girls'. The Women's Army Auxiliary Corps was founded on 28 March. Their purpose was to act as clerks, telephonists, motor cyclists, cooks and waitresses, both on the home front as well as overseas. By the end of the war, some 57,000 women had served with the organization.

On 11 March, Baghdad which in 1917 was the southern capital of the Ottoman Empire, was captured by British forces under the command of Lieutenant General Sir Frederick Stanley Maude, who had become the Commander of Allied Forces in Mesopotamia in July 1916.

General Maude died of cholera on 18 November 1917 in Baghdad and is buried in the city's North Gate War Cemetery.

One of the most significant events of the First World War took place on 6 April, when American President, Woodrow Wilson, took the decision to declare war on Germany. America had a large German population and many Americans were in favour of remaining neutral, but after German U-boats began targeting neutral shipping – a policy which saw America lose five of its merchant ships in March 1917 alone – a declaration of war quickly followed.

The Battle of Arras took place between 9 April and 16 May, and was a strategically important offensive on German-held positions in and around the French town of Arras. Units from Australia, Canada, Great Britain, Newfoundland and New Zealand took part in the attack. Even though the subsequent battle was hailed as an Allied victory, at its end the combined casualties were 158,000, whilst the German figures were estimated at around 125,000.

Overnight on 6 May, Germany dropped the first bomb from a fixed wing aircraft whilst on a mission to London. One person was killed in the attack.

The first day of Battle of Messines in Flanders, 7 June, saw British forces detonate nineteen mines under the German trenches, the contents of which contained ammonium nitrate mixed with aluminium powder. So powerful was the resulting explosion, that an estimated 10,000 German soldiers were killed. It remains to this day, the deadliest intentional man-made explosion of a non-nuclear bomb.

Lieutenant General Sir Frederick Stanley Maude, 1917.

On 17 July, King George V officially changed the Royal surname to that of Windsor from the more Germanic sounding name of Saxe-Coburg Gotha. On the same day Winston Churchill became Minister of Munitions.

The Third Battle of Ypres took place between 31 July and 10 November. On 22 July, in the build up to the battle, the British threw a total of 4,250,000 grenades at the German lines. On 6 November in a landscape shattered by shell fire and pockmarked with mud-filled shell holes, Canadian forces finally succeeded in capturing the Passchendaele Ridge. The Official History records 244,897 men of the British forces killed in this attritional battle which came to symbolize the horror and futility of the war.

On 2 August, Edwin Harris Dunning DSO, who was a Squadron Commander with the British Royal Naval Air Service, became the first man to land an aircraft on a ship when he landed his Sopwith Pup on the deck of HMS *Furious* at Scapa Flow. Sadly he died five days later whilst attempting the same feat. His aircraft ended up in the sea, with him being knocked unconscious as it hit the water. He drowned still strapped in to his cockpit.

A Dover man at Cambrai

Miss L. Johnson of 38 Albany Place, Dover, received a letter from her brother, Gunner B. Johnson, who was serving with the 28th Brigade, Royal Field Artillery, 5th Division, II Army Corps. The letter was dated 15 September.

'No doubt you wonder why I have not written before. Well, it has been a hard job to get anything. We have been away from England for five weeks. We get no money, so we cannot buy anything, not even paper to write on. We are going on all right as regards food. I am quite well. The weather was very hot when first we got here, but has changed this week to rain. I must not say where we are. I was at the battle three weeks ago today [Cambrai], and was very lucky to come out without being hurt, twenty-two being killed and wounded in our battery. Of course, I will let you know more if ever I arrive home. If mother could send me a couple of packets of cigarettes I should be very thankful. If you send things in parcels, they are broken open before we get them, and you had best send them in the centre of a newspaper, so I give you the tip to avoid theft.'

The Battle of Jerusalem took place between 17 November and 30 December. It was a victory for the British and Dominion forces under the command of General Edmund Allenby. Ottoman forces who were defending the Holy City, decided to surrender it to Allenby rather than risk its destruction by Allied artillery.

As the year came to an end, so in effect did the Russian Empire.

Tsar Nicholas ll had been forced to abdicate on 15 March 1917 and was initially replaced by a provisional government of the Russian Republic, made up of ten members with a further eight being added the following month. Eight months later, on 8 November 1917 the provisional government was removed and replaced with a Bolshevik/ Communist government. The following March saw the Bolshevik leaders signing the Treaty of Brest-Litovsk with Germany on 3 March 1918, which effectively ended Russia's involvement in the First World War, but it came at a hefty price, which included ceding certain areas to Germany, Austria and the Ottoman Empire, as well as agreeing to pay Germany reparations to the tune of six million German gold marks.

Life in Dover 1917

The story of Dover in 1917 is clearly going to centre around the war and its effects on the lives of the people in the town. It was a year that nobody would look back on in years to come with any sense of pleasure. People reading about those desperate times today will do so through different eyes and with a totally different perspective. No matter how the words used to describe Dover during the dark days of the First World War are written, they will still be read in double quick time, no matter how well intentioned and genuine the interest is. The only people who can truly appreciate and properly understand those days are the ones who lived through them.

Despite all the scares and actual dangers that the war brought with it, Dover escaped quite lightly. The casualty list of those who were killed as a direct result of the war, both civilian and military personnel, numbered only twelve. But there were other incidents which affected the town during those years, and were evidence of how the trials, tribulations and heartbreak that are associated with war, are echoed, to a lesser degree, by happenings on the home front, in the everyday normality of life.

The tram accident on Crabble Hill Road on the afternoon of Sunday, 24 August resulted in the deaths of eleven people with another sixty injured. It was the worst disaster to befall Dover and the most serious tram accident that there had ever been.

The River Light Railway Company which owned the trams, had

been operating in the town since 2 October 1905. The trams in question were double deckers which ran on a single track and were driven by two 25hp motors. They were fitted with ordinary hand brakes, electric rheostatic brakes and the Spencer slipper track brake.

The gradient on Crabble Road was one in ten-and-a-half at the steepest part of the road. A tram that was travelling down the road on the northward bound part of the journey, had to stop at the junction of London Road. Because of the steepness of the road, the tram was only supposed to be travelling at a maximum speed of four miles per hour and the track brake had to be applied before leaving the junction at the top of the road. The driver of the tram at the time of the accident was Albert Bissenden, who had only been working for the company since 21 July 1917. He had applied for the position of a motor man, and was placed under the tutelage of an experienced driving instructor to learn the drive the trams. He was looked upon as a more than adequate candidate.

Albert James Bissenden was an ex-military man having served as a Private (5998) with the Army Ordnance Corps, initially enlisting on 15 June 1907 at Dover, just before his nineteenth birthday. After having completed his three years' service on 14 June 1910, he was placed on the Army Reserve.

The River Light Railway Company was aware of Bissenden's military past and the fact that he had been medically discharged from the Army on 1 June 1917, for having experienced what the newspapers of the day reported as, a nervous breakdown. There were other differences between what was written in the *Dover Express* and what was actually documented on his Army Pension papers.

Whilst he was undergoing his training to be a tram driver, he was under the watchful eye of Driver Brett, who had ten to fifteen years' experience of driving trams. Bissenden was under Brett's tutelage for nine days, during which time it was recorded by Brett that Bissenden showed no signs of nervousness and judged that he would be likely to prove a good motor man. Bissenden took a tram out on his own for the first time on 16 August when he went out on the River track, and by the time of the accident he had driven the route for four days. Brett added that he thought Bissenden to be a man of excellent character and if he had not felt he was good enough he would not have let him go out

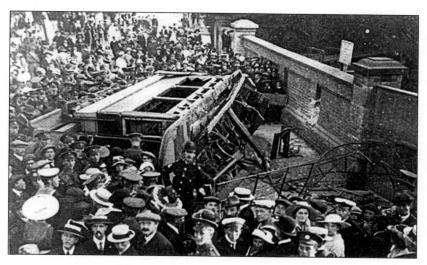

Tram number 20 soon after the crash

on his own. Bissenden was also watched and closely observed by the company's electrician, Mr Bond, who was ultimately responsible for passing Bissenden as being suitable to drive the trams.

An inquiry into the accident and subsequent deaths began at 2.30pm on 24 August, at Dover Town Hall. It was chaired by Colonel Pringle and also present and part of the board of inquiry, were the Mayor, Mr Farley, Brigadier General Bickford, Brigadier General Massey-Lloyd, Alderman Prescott, Councillors Beaufoy, Barwick, Morgan, Gatehouse, Barnes, Hobday and Leney, the Town Clerk, Mr Knocker, the Tramways Manager, Mr Carden and the Electrical Engineer, Mr Woodman.

Colonel Pringle, in opening the inquiry, expressed the sympathy of the President of the Board of Trade and his own sympathy with the relatives of those who were killed and injured.

Local bye-laws stated the maximum number of passengers that the trams could lawfully carry, although the conductors, who were ultimately responsible for the numbers on the trams, could allow more passengers on whilst the tram was travelling on a flat section of the track, but when travelling along the more difficult River section of track, there was a strict instruction that no more passengers were allowed on the tram than the seating capacity allowed for. This was twenty-two inside and twenty-six outside. There should have only been a total of forty-eight passengers on the tram at the time of the accident, but there were in fact seventy, twenty-two more than should have been allowed. Eleven were killed and a further fifty-nine were injured.

Mr Carden explained that the responsibility for allowing more passengers would normally be with the conductress, who at the time of the accident, was Charlotte Scrase, but she was sadly one of those who had been killed. She was 27 years of age. Before the war Charlotte had lived at 80 Heathfield Avenue, Dover, with her mother, also called Charlotte, her two younger sisters, Maud and Edith, along with her elder brother, Arthur. (There are three men with the name Arthur Scrase recorded as having served in the Army during the First World War, one with the Royal Engineers, one with Queen's (Royal West Surrey) Regiment and another who was with the East Surrey Regiment. Which, if any of them, is Charlotte's brother, is not known.)

Another regulation in relation to the trams was that passengers were not allowed to stand on the top deck in addition to the seating capacity, through concern that there could be too great a weight load, which could end up being dangerous. To ensure that this rule was enforced by the conductress, an Inspector was placed at a strategic location along the route of the tram journey at Buckland. The inspector on duty at the time of the accident was Inspector Elgay, although he stated that he did not recall seeing the tram go past him on that day.

Each day before the trams took to the roads they were inspected by the depot mechanic. The tram that was involved in the crash was from the Buckland Depot and the mechanic there was a Mr Nye. When he gave evidence to the inquiry, he confirmed that he had worked for the company for fourteen years and that at Buckland he looked after fifteen trams, ten of which ran every day. He inspected tram number twenty, the one that had been involved in the crash, before it left the depot on that fateful morning and confirmed that everything was as should be.

One of the people who gave evidence to the inquiry was Laura Bomford, who lived at 13 Park Avenue, Dover, and who had been a passenger on tram number twenty. The following paragraphs of what she told the inquiry are how they appeared in the *Dover Express* newspaper dated Friday, 24 August.

'Miss Laura Bomford of 13 Park Avenue, stated that she was a

passenger on the car and was riding inside, at first standing and then securing a seat on the right-hand side, about the centre. She heard the conductress at St Bartholomew's Church, tell the driver to go straight on, as the car was full up. At London Road she was sure that no one was standing up inside, but there were some people in the doorway, and on the lower platform there were two, if not more, standing. On the driver's platform there might have been a soldier leaning up against the door. She could not be sure that the car stopped at the top, but her impression was that it did not. She could not say how many passengers were on the top. Immediately after turning the corner it struck her that the car was out of control. She did not realise before. She saw at this moment a soldier go out of the door, which was open on to the driver's platform, and take hold of one of the handles. She could not say whether the driver was on the platform or not. That was before the arch. She did not notice anything unusual in the behaviour of the driver before that. She knew the road very well, and realised that they must go into the wall at the bottom, but she had no impression of the car going over slowly. She was surprised that there was not a violent crash against the wall. The car overturned so smoothly that her head was not bumped violently, and what she felt more was the people falling on her. She felt the car tilting slowly whilst it was moving forward. She also had a clear impression of the car moving along the ground on its side some four or five yards. She could not say whether the regulation of four miles an hour was obeyed, as she seldom went to River in a car.'

Other witnesses gave their versions of what they remembered. One of them, a Mrs Clark, who lived on Crabble Hill, stated that the tram did not stop at the top of the hill, but instead passed over the brow at a higher speed than usual. Mrs Clark and her son were miraculously uninjured, other than some minor bruises.

Fred John Cook told the inquiry that he had been employed on the tramways for nineteen years, and had driven trams for most of that time, although now he was employed as a clerk in the tramways office. He arrived at the scene of the accident just before 4pm, and was asked by Mr Carden to look through the overturned tram and recover any of the passengers' property that he could find. When he got to the front of the tram he noticed that the controller handles were full open to drive ahead. The small handle was in the ahead position and the power handle was in the full speed position. He hadn't seen anybody near the handles. He said that there was a remote chance that the handles could be in the positions that they were as a result of the accident, but that nothing was touching or was wedged up against them. They should have been in an off position. If he had been trying to apply the emergency brake, the small handle should have been in the emergency position, and if trying to reverse, in the reverse position. The position of the handles as he found them in, indicated that the current was in use when the tram was going down the hill, which should not have been the case.

Mr Cook further commented that the rheostatic brake was for use in an emergency when it was required to bring the tram to a sudden stop. From the position of the brake handles as he had seen them when he walked through the tram, he could tell that the driver had not used the rheostatic brakes whilst the tram had been careering down the hill.

Albert James Bissenden survived the accident and gave evidence to the inquiry. He started off by going through his experience as a tram driver, how long he had worked for the company and what duty he had been working on the day of the accident. He then gave a lengthy description of his actions leading up to taking the tram over the brow of the hill. It was after this point that his testimony became really interesting:

> 'I went over the top of the brow and threw off the controller, but found that the handbrake would not stop the car. I knocked the "dog" in and tried to screw down the slipper brake. By that time the car was gathering speed round the corner. Finding that it would not hold, I then put my hand to my emergency brake, but I could not get it back, as it was jammed hard and fast. The handle of the hand brake seemed to turn easily, and met with no resistance. I came to the conclusion that the hand brake would not pull up the car, as usually I had only to give one turn. As I found that I could do nothing else I jumped off just before I reached the arch over the roadway.'

It was incredible to read that Bissenden had actually jumped off the tram whilst it was careering down the hill and with his co-worker and so many passengers, all still on board, all of whom looked to him as the driver to help keep them safe on their journey.

At such moments in time, history often records feats of heroism that are above and beyond what would normally be expected of any human being. Crabble Hill in Dover on 19 August 1917 was to be no different. The hero on this occasion came in the form of Walter George Gunner, who was an off duty Trooper (5620) with the 1st Battalion, Dragoon Guards. At the time he was attached to the Army Pay Corps, and later transferred and became a Corporal (12969), serving with them in Dover.

Bissenden had tried to apply the tram's emergency brake but it had not worked as the power was still on, but Bissenden had for some reason failed to notice this. He then tried the tram's slipper brakes, but this did not work either. Not to be deterred and with the tram gathering speed down the hill, Bissenden then tried the hand brake, but that did not work. This was where Walter George Gunner stepped up and became a real hero, but not in a way that he might have envisaged when he enlisted in the Army. Have watched Bissenden struggle to bring the tram under control by trying to deploy the different brakes, he tried to stop the tram himself by using his feet as emergency brakes. Walter became one of the injured passengers himself when he lost both his feet as a result of his heroic efforts that day. He was later awarded the Albert Medal for his bravery and self-sacrifice in trying to stop the tram.

Back at the inquiry, Bissenden was bombarded with different questions from members of the inquiry team and some of his answers could only be described as contradictory with the evidence provided by others who had told their individual stories to the inquiry.

The inquest in to the deaths of eleven of the tram's passengers, opened on 21 August, and was heard by the Coroner, Sydenham Payne. It was adjourned until 27 August. After the jury had heard all the evidence they retired to make their decision, and after only forty-five minutes they returned. The jury foreman, James Wood, announced their verdict that the accident was due to an error of judgement by the driver of the tram, Albert James Bissenden, who was too inexperienced to have been at the controls.

Remarkably Bissenden was never charged with any criminal offence in relation to the incident, although he had to live with the memories of that fateful day for the rest of his life.

Blissenden's British Army pension record does not show that he had suffered from a nervous breakdown as was recorded in the newspapers of the time, but more on that shortly. After having been placed on the Army Reserve on 14 June 1910, after serving his three years with the Colours, he was twice struck off its strength, on 8 June 1912 and again in 1913. On both occasions it was for failing to 'render his Life Certificate'. With the outbreak of war he re-joined as a private in the Army Ordnance Corps on 10 August 1914 whilst in New Zealand, but returned to the United Kingdom by the end of November that year, where he remained for the following year. During this time he was stationed at Colchester in Essex where he was utilized as a carpenter and an orderly. His time in the town wasn't without incident, as he was twice disciplined, on 25 May 1915, for causing a disturbance after a night out, when he used bad language to an NCO. The second incident took place a month later on 11 June, when he was absent from his department duty and found in a nearby pub.

Albert married Mabel Minnie Reeves on 12 December 1915 at St Bartholomew's Parish Church in Charlton by Dover. Mabel was a local girl, who lived at 2 Washington Villas, Monis Road in Dover.

On 11 January 1916 he arrived at Alexandria in Egypt as part of the Egyptian Expeditionary Force, and was stationed in Cairo where he was a storeman. He had been there for less than a month when he was in trouble again. This time for being absent from his Depot duty, his punishment was the deduction of one day's pay. Whilst serving in Cairo Albert became unwell and had a short stay in hospital so that he could be thoroughly examined and a determination could be made as to what was wrong with him. He was diagnosed as having Neurasthenia, an ill-defined medical condition which was characterised by such ailments as fatigue, headaches, irritability, apathy, drowsiness and loss of memory. He was invalided home from Egypt, leaving there on 10 February on board the hospital ship HMHS *Letitia*, and after a twelve-day journey, arrived back in England on 22 February.

On 1 May Albert was examined at the Bermondsey Military Hospital, which was situated in Ladywell Road, Lewisham. He was further diagnosed as also suffering with Vasomotor Disturbance, which relates to the body's nervous system, causing blood vessels to constrict and dilate, which can in turn lead to imbalance.

Viewing this situation through today's eyes it does seem incredible that any person having been diagnosed with the ailments that Albert Bissenden had, could have conceivably been given such a job. What is even more remarkable is that on 15 August 1917, four days before the tragic accident, Albert was examined by a doctor in Dover, when it was noted that his heart action was rapid, and that although there was an improvement in his condition, he was still suffering with fifty per cent disablement.

It is inconceivable to believe that if the River Light Railway Company had known of this information they would have allowed him to drive a tram.

Dover's political picture changed somewhat during the war, when it ceased to be a parliamentary borough, as a result of a Bill that was passed through Parliament, changing it to a County Division, which comprised Dover Borough, Deal Borough, Walmer Urban District, and Dover and Eastry Rural District. The district had a very large electorate as the age of males who were entitled to vote had been extended; women who were thirty years of age and above, were also entitled to vote.

The exact area of the new district was settled at an enquiry which was held at Maidstone on July 19, at which the bigger Dover Corporation were represented. For some reason the members of that group chose not to make too much of a fight out of saving Dover as a solitary Parliamentary Borough, possibly because they realized their efforts would be futile.

Politics on a more local level was also affected in relation to the Municipal Wards of Dover, which Dover Council decided could be divided into six wards with one person representing each ward rather than three wards with two members representing each ward.

All of Dover's municipal elections were suspended from 1914 for the duration of the war, which meant that the Mayor, Councillor Farley, was re-elected for a fourth year in succession on 1 November

1918. This was a record that had only been equalled once before, some 400 years earlier. Some in the town held the view that during such a momentous time as the First World War stability was all important, and that it was not desirable to make changes in the office of its Mayor and of the other seats on the Council. The town's Member of Parliament, Lord Duncannon, had announced in August of 1917 that he was leaving the Unionist Party to join the newly formed National Party.

Other events in Dover during 1917 which affected the public as a whole, included the cost of tram fares doubling in price. After losing so many of their experienced drivers to the war, and with the tragic accident of 19 August, most people found it hard to understand why.

The building of air raid shelters to protect the people of Dover from German Zeppelins and Gotha bombers, which the government had left to the town councils to arrange, had not been progressed as quickly as might have been expected. It was 22 August before the people of Dover saw any German aircraft in the skies above them, on this occasion it was in the shape of Gotha bombers during a daytime raid. This turned out to be the last daytime raid over England, due no doubt to new and powerful anti-aircraft batteries which had been set up across Kent and Essex. On 2 September the town experienced a moonlight raid, when Gotha aircraft dropped bombs on the town which resulted in the death of one civilian.

The war had affected both the town of Dover as well as its people in so many different ways. The local roads were generally in a poor state of repair, because of the lack of sufficient materials to repair them. The tramway system, which so many people living and working in Dover relied upon to get them about the town, had to resort to digging up sections of rail from the River section, to be able to repair other parts of the tramway track.

The Dover Harbour Board had continued to struggle throughout 1917. With the war came an end to revenue from general trade, as the only vessels using the harbour were military related ones. The Board's only source of income was from the salvage work done by its tug boats. The problem was despite having earned very little in the way of money, they still had financial outgoings to maintain their fleet of ships and staff to sail and maintain them. That they had actually survived at all was only down to being able to secure large loans from the Treasury, which would ultimately cripple the future existence of the Harbour Board, unless their repayment could be re-negotiated.

One area where the town appeared not to have struggled, was in house and property sales, which although not having sold at a premium, had nonetheless sold in some numbers.

Tilmanstone and Snowdon collieries had worked steadily throughout the year, both mines producing just short of 3,000 tons of much needed coal, each week throughout the year.

The town's Royal Victoria Hospital had also struggled financially. With so much more expected of it in a time of war, and having to deal with a reduction in staff, still providing a comprehensive day to day service to the general public was no easy task. The hospital's finance committee had to deal effectively with their financial situation, whilst the Dover Trades and Labour Council had tried to organise a weekly levy for the hospital amongst the town's workers, but with only partial success.

By the end of 1917, Dover, like most communities across the nation, had experienced its fair share of pain and suffering in the amount of its sons that had been lost in the war. There were few local families who had men serving in the armed forces, who had not lost someone, their only solace and comfort coming from the knowledge that they had served with honour and had undertaken their duty bravely.

During the same period the people of Dover had experienced the war at first hand in the form of Zeppelin raids on the town and across the county. In the early hours of 21 April the residents of Dover had been woken up by the sound of exploding shells, as the town came under attack from six German destroyers. In only four minutes, some sixty shells rained down on the town but remarkably there was not one single casualty. Bravely two Royal Navy destroyers, HMS *Swift* and HMS *Broke*, engaged the more heavily armed German vessels, sinking two of them and seeing off the other four. This victory came at a cost, with twenty-two British sailors killed. Together with the bodies of twenty-eight German sailors, they were brought back to Dover. HMS *Broke,* which had sunk the two German destroyers returned to the safety of Dover Harbour, and a hero's welcome on her arrival.

The *Dover Express* reported that the fifty dead sailors from both nations, were initially laid out in Market Hall, before being buried in St James Cemetery, with full military honours afforded to all, but the Commonwealth War Graves Commission shows only seven British sailors who were killed on 21 April are buried in the cemetery. They were:

Leading Stoker Charles Ernest Dart
Stoker Robert Donnelly
Stoker 2nd Class William Foxhall
Signalman Walter Hawkins Lockett
Stoker 1st Class James Joseph Rafferty
Ordinary Seaman Robert Victor Towers
Able Seaman George Tubb
Stoker Donnelly was from the crew of HMS *Swift* whilst all of the others were from HMS *Broke*.

Having checked the other cemetery records for Dover, no Navy personnel were buried in them who had been killed on 21 April 1917.

Further raids were carried out on Dover by the German Imperial Navy, but they had stopped by the end of the month.

There was a food campaign in Dover underway during 1917. Not surprisingly, it was about getting people to eat less and grow more of their own food so that they could become more self-sufficient. This was achieved not by scaremongering speeches, but by the cold realities of war. In the late spring of 1917, the potato crop gave out, and with the intensified German submarine campaign in full flow, people of Dover began to fully appreciate the threat that they were now facing.

As the year continued, more and more food items started to become scarce. These included tea, sugar and butter, which placed an even greater demand on margarine supplies. In an effort to try and alleviate the food related shortages, the Dover Food Production Committee was formed. One of the first things that they did was to make available more ground for allotments in the town so as to encourage residents to grow their own vegetables, including potatoes. This campaign resulted in a very large potato crop for Dover. The arrival of autumn saw the setting up locally of the Food Control Committee, which consisted mainly of labour representatives. It had been put in place to deal with the issue of sugar cards. It also managed to acquire sufficient milk for the town, albeit at a higher price that they had wanted to pay.

Throughout the year the Military Service Tribunals had been kept busy in Dover, as more and more men tried to avoid enlisting in the armed forces. Although many of those who appeared before the Tribunals were genuine claimants, some undoubtedly were not. With many already having lost friends and family in the war and with lists of the dead and wounded appearing more frequently in the newspapers in larger and larger numbers, maybe for some it was down to a feeling of foreboding of the fate that would befall them if they enlisted.

Obituaries were sadly an everyday occurrence with or without war, and Dover lost its fair share of well-known local individuals throughout the year. Here are just a few of them:

Mr W. Baker, Church Warden at St Mary's Church. Died 2 January.

Mr F.C. Bartholomew, died 12 January.

Madame Minnie Curtis. Died 20 January.

Captain G.W.W. Paine. Formerly of South Eastern and Chatham Railway Marine Service. Died 20 January.

Mr H. Coleman. Aged 91 years. Died 24 February.

Colonel R.W.C. Winsloe. A defender of Potchefstroom in the Boer War 1881. Died 31 May.

The Reverend E.R. Orger, MA. The vicar of Hougham for 22 years. Aged 90 years. Died 4 June.

Lady Dickeson. Widow of the late Sir Richard Dickeson. Died 28 June.

Captain Palliser, JP. Died 13 July.

Dr Morrison. Died 15 July.

Mr W.P. Hampton, of Langdon Abbey. Died 16 July.

Mr G. Spicer. Owner of the *Dover Standard* newspaper. Died 2 October.

Mr R.R. Gutsole, Member of the Dover Board of Guardians. Died 23 October.

Mr G. Forster. Died 25 October.

Mr H. Meadows. Died 28 October.

The Reverend W.R. Mowll. Died 2 December.

Christmas Day at the Dover Union Workhouse had seldom seen such peace and quiet on its premises as it did in 1917. The reason for this was a simple one. All of the children had been packed off to Brighton during the festive celebrations, leaving the adults on their own. Roast beef was served up for Christmas dinner, but the Workhouse inmates had to make do with Tapioca pudding instead of the traditional Christmas pudding, but they weren't complaining. In the afternoon an abundance of little extras were provided such as, apples, oranges, sweets, nuts and tobacco.

Members of the Board of Guardians who ran the Workhouse were present for the Christmas dinner. These included its Chairman, Alderman C.J. Sellens. Mr J. Parsons, Mr Pointer, Dr Elliot, Mr Hookway, Mr and Mrs Harvey, and Mr Fagg.

CHAPTER SIX

1918 - The Final Push

On 23 April 1918 the British Royal Navy carried out a daring day time raid on the German held port of Zeebrugge on the coast of Belgium, the location being the home base for German submarines. After the raid the British authorities took full advantage of the propaganda value of what was seen as a successful raid. It certainly managed to boost morale amongst their own men as well helping to maintain the public sense of wellbeing and pride in the effectiveness of the Royal Navy. But was it as successful as has been claimed?

The original idea for the audacious operation came from Lord Jellicoe, although Vice Admiral Sir Roger Keyes was one of those subsequently tasked with its planning and implementation. It has been described as one of the best-conceived operations, not only of the war, but in British naval history. On the day of the attack, Sir Roger was in command of a fleet of 168 ships and some 1,800 men, whose intention it was to block the port by sinking ships across the entrance and exit to the harbour so preventing German U-boats from leaving.

Although simplistic in its idea and execution, the idea itself had first been put forward as early as October 1914, which then beggars the question as to why it subsequently took three-and-a-half years to make it a reality. Even then

HMS Vindictive

HMS Intrepid *and HMS* Iphigenia *after the Zeebrugge raid*

the operation did not totally go according to plan. It was postponed on at least two occasions, once on 11 April 1918 when the attacking convoy of ships had to stop and turn back because of inclement and worsening weather. Two specific elements that were needed for the operation to be able to take place, were for the wind to be blowing in the right direction and a calm sea. One part of the plan was the deployment of a thick smoke screen to blind the Germans to what was coming their way, providing the Royal Navy with the ability to carry out their plan before they had time to react. The calm sea was needed so that the small motor boats that were part of the attacking convoy, would be able to pick up the crews of the ships that had been used to blockade the port.

As well as other English ports along the south and south-east coastline, Dover was heavily involved with providing vessels and manpower to take part in the operation.

The following passage is taken from the book by J.B. Firth, *Dover and the Great War* about the raid at Zeebrugge, which was first published in 1919.

> 'The general idea was to block the two submarine nests and close the double exits and entrances of the Bruges Canal, particularly at Zeebrugge, which was the more important of the two. Six old cruisers, filled with concrete, were to be sunk in the channels at Zeebrugge and Ostend as near the dock gates as possible, and the special work assigned to the Vindictive was to land Marines on the curving Mole at Zeebrugge, who were to engage the attention of the shore batteries while the block ships slipped in, and to destroy as far as possible all the sheds, hangars and stores which were situated upon the Mole. It was plainly essential that the two flotillas should arrive simultaneously, so that neither port could warn the other and success or failure might obviously depend on a momentary shifting of the wind. The whole expedition was a sort of forlorn hope on a heroic scale, and it was entrusted to volunteers who had been invited to offer themselves for a specially hazardous enterprise. These were so numerous that it had to be left to a ballot to decide who should go, and the crew of the Intrepid, refused in a body to leave their ship, when told to make way for newcomers. Such was the spirit of those who set out to twist the dragon's tail.
>
> "St George for England!" was the signal which Admiral Keyes made in the destroyer Warwick, in which he flew his flag. "May we give the dragon's tail a dammed good twist!" was the answer of Captain Carpenter, in the Vindictive.'

The other problem that the British had to contend with was the strength of the defences they were against. These included mine fields, machine guns and heavy artillery. The Germans had also recognized the importance of Zeebrugge and Ostend, and turned them into extremely formidable defensive positions so that their submarines and destroyers could maintain a substantive threat in both the North Sea and the English Channel. In essence it was their very existence which determined that any assault on the harbour needed to be in the main a seaborne raid, rather than solely the landing of a large infantry force, which undoubtedly would have sustained extremely high casualties and resulted in the overall failure of the mission.

The bulk of the flotilla which set off on the operation, did so from the harbour at Dover, leaving there at 4pm in broad daylight. One of these ships was HMS *Vindictive*, which had undergone extensive alterations in preparation for the attack. In particular her weaponry had been greatly increased which turned her into a mobile killing machine. Her decks were now crammed with howitzers, pom-pom guns, Lewis guns, two 6-inch guns, a flame-thrower and Stokes mortars.

Having arrived off the Belgian coast, it was the job of the much smaller motor-boats to activate the smoke screen which would then allow the relevant vessels of the flotilla to remain unseen by the German defenders for as long as possible. This tactic was so successful, that HMS *Vindictive* was able to get within 300 yards of the coast, before they were spotted. Her job was that of an assault ship and as such she had to head towards the end of the Mole and disembark her landing parties so that they could engage the German defensive positions, and provide sufficient time for the three intended blocking ships to reach their required positions before they were sunk.

As the *Vindictive* approached the far end of the Mole at one minute past midnight, she prepared to disembark her two landing parties. Initially the seamen's landing party was led by Captain H.C. Halahan and the Royal Marines were led by Lieutenant Colonel B.H. Elliot and his second in command, Major A.A. Cordner. Almost immediately all three men were killed by ferocious German machine-gun fire. So intense was the German firepower that the *Vindictive* very quickly had some of her howitzers and flame-throwers destroyed, as well as sustaining damage to her superstructure.

Three minutes behind *Vindictive*, HMS *Daffodil* arrived; her job was to push the *Vindictive* tight up against the Mole and then, along with HMS *Iris* which was close behind her, she had to disembark her landing parties so that they could support those men from *Vindictive* who were already ashore and in the thick of things.

The *Vindictive*'s heroic assault took up so much of the Germans' attention that two of the ships that were to be used to block the entrance to the inner harbour, were able to reach their intended targets. Despite this the raid was not a success. The sunken British vessels did not manage to block the entrance sufficiently to prevent the Germans from being able to manoeuvre their ships and submarines in and out of the harbour.

HMS Vindictive *following the raid at Zeebrugge*

Vice Admiral Sir Roger Keyes sent a report dated 19 February 1919 to the Lord Commissioners of the Admiralty, which contained 123 points, concerning the raids at Zeebrugge and Ostend on 22 and 23 April 1918 and the subsequent raid at Ostend, seventeen days later on 10 May 1918.

Point eleven of the report included the following:

'Our operations were completely successful in attaining their first and most important objective. The entrance to the Bruges shipping canal was blocked. The second objective, the blocking of the entrance to Ostend harbour, was not achieved.'

The first part of that statement is not factually correct. Only two out of the three intended blocking vessels were actually sunk inside the inner wall of the harbour, but as has been explained earlier in this chapter, the Germans were able to dredge out a new channel, which by-passed the sunken blocking vessels, and it was not too long before the harbour was up and running again, allowing the German vessels to come and go as they needed to.

It depends on how success is measured and what form it takes, before a true decision can be made as to whether something was or is deemed to have been successful. The raid on Zeebrugge if looked at purely from the perspective of whether it achieved its objective of blocking the port, then the answer has to be no, it did not. If measured by the number of men killed or wounded and the number of vessels that were lost, then it could only be considered a total and absolute defeat for the British. They lost one destroyer, HMS *North Star*, 227 men killed and a further 356 who were wounded. Compared to the German losses of only eight men dead and sixteen wounded, it was no contest. If on the other hand it is measured by men's bravery and a dogged determination to get the job done, no matter what the cost, coupled with the positive effect those collective acts had on morale or the public's perception that it was a job well done, then it was a resounding success.

The British authorities somehow managed to turn what some observers were calling a disaster, into a total success – a classic example of how to use propaganda.

On 28 April 1918, nine men who had lost their lives as a result of the raid on Zeebrugge, were buried at St James Cemetery, Dover. A large

St James Cemetery, Dover

number of people had turned out to watch the procession of the coffins of these brave young men, as they slowly made their way through the streets of the town, on their way to the cemetery. The names of these nine men are also inscribed on a cross which is located in the grounds of the cemetery. There is another memorial to all of those who died in the raid, in the shape of the Zeebrugge Bell and memorial plaque which can be found in the town hall at Dover.

It has to be remembered that everybody who took part in the raid, did so voluntarily in the knowledge that there was a more than fair chance that they might not survive. The raid on Zeebrugge lasted for approximately an hour and during that time so many men carried out acts of bravery that 585 of them were awarded medals for their actions during the course of 22 and 23 April 1918. That means that one in three men received awards, a truly remarkable feat, making the raid at Zeebrugge one of the most highly decorated in modern warfare.

The Victoria Cross: six were awarded initially, with a further at a later date.

The Most Honourable Order of the Bath, (2nd Class, Knight Commander): one was awarded.

The Most Honourable Order of the Bath, (3rd Class, a Companion): four were awarded.

The Most Distinguished Order of St Michael & St George: two were awarded.

The Distinguished Service Order: twenty were awarded.

Bar to the Distinguished Service Order: only one was awarded.

The Distinguished Service Cross: a total of twenty-seven were awarded initially, with a further one at a later date.

Bar to the Distinguished Service Cross: two were awarded.

The Conspicuous Gallantry Medal: sixteen were awarded.

The Distinguished Service Medal: 140 were awarded initially, with a further two at a later date.

Bar to the Distinguished Service Medal: three were awarded initially, with a further three at a later date.

Mentioned in Despatches: 268 men were awarded this distinction.

Fifty-six officers and men were promoted as a direct result of their involvement in the raid.

The *Croix de Guerre* (France): nineteen were awarded.

The Order of Leopold (Belgium): two were awarded.

The *Légion d'Honneur* (France): ten were awarded.

Dover certainly played her part in the raids, with the following vessels having set out on the raid from the safety of the town's harbour: HMS *Vindictive, Iris II, Daffodil, Thetis, Intrepid, Iphigenia, Sirius, Brilliant, Phoebe, North Star, Trident, Mansfield, Whirlwind, Myngs, Velox, Morris, Moorsom, Melpomene, Tempest, Tetrarch*, and the flag ship of the Vice Admiral, Sir Roger Keyes, HMS *Warwick*.

There was also a picket boat, whose job it was to pick up the crew members of the British submarines C1 and C2, the Minesweeper, HMS *Lingfield*, thirteen coastal motor boats as well as thirty-three motor launches.

HMS *Erebus* and HMS *Terror* were used to bombard the area of Zeebrugge in support of the British raid, whilst HMS *Attentive, Scott, Ullswater, Teazer* and *Stork*, had the job of patrolling off Zeebrugge, to ensure that the flotilla was not attacked from the rear by German vessels.

Undeterred by the failings of the initial raid at Ostend on the evening of 22/23 April, a second raid went ahead on 10 May. On the initial raid the plan had been to sink two blocking ships at the mouth of the canal at Ostend, but for a combination of reasons the operation was a complete failure.

Having already played a significant part in the initial raid on Zeebrugge, *Vindictive* played an even more important part at Ostend.

The date for the second raid was 9 May 1918. If successful the submarines and destroyers which Germany had stationed at Brugges could effectively be trapped and prevented from wreaking further havoc in the English Channel.

If Britain were to have any chance of securing the English Channel from the threat caused by the German U-boats to Allied shipping in that area, then they needed to neutralize the problem. The fact that in April and May 1918 Britain was still carrying out operations specifically targeted at locations such as Zeebrugge and Ostend, which in turn required the allocation of so much time, money, effort, equipment and man power, showed just how serious a problem these ports in German hands, posed to Britain. If German naval operations could be curtailed there, particularly those of their submarines, they would then have no

HMS Vindictive *after having been sunk off Ostend*

other alternative but to move to other locations further away from the English Channel, which would greatly hinder their effectiveness whilst at the same time making them more vulnerable.

The plan for the May attack was approved by Admiral Sir Roger Keyes and his second in command, Commodore Hubert Lynes. The ability for the British to carry out another attack was greatly simplified as in essence it replicated the previous attempt on the evening of 22/23 April: a smoke screen out at sea to hide the vessels undertaking the raid from the German defensive positions, which were on the receiving end of an artillery bombardment. It was hoped this would be a sufficient distraction to allow the British vessels more time to secure their objective.

This time the British raiding party was not coming out of Dover which not only greatly reduced the time and distance they had to travel, it also meant less chance of being discovered en route. The British ships left from Dunkirk but the operation suffered an early setback when with the raiding party was underway: HMS *Sappho*, which was to be one of the blocking ships at Ostend, had to turn back to Dunkirk, after suffering an explosion in her boiler room. Despite now only having HMS *Vindictive* as a blocking ship, the decision was made to continue with the attack.

The *Vindictive* had been repaired after her previous involvement in the raid on Zeebrugge, where she sustained significant damage, but the repairs were minimal. In the knowledge of how this proud old lady of the seas was going to finish her days, all of her unessential equipment was removed and her ballast tanks were filled with concrete, to make it harder for the Germans to be able to move her after she had been sunk. She was commanded by Alfred Godsal, whose job it was to sail the *Vindictive* into position and sink her. He was ably assisted by six officers and a crew of forty-eight, every one of them a volunteer, most of whom had served on HMS *Brilliant* of the raids on 22/23 April.

In support of the *Vindictive* were seventeen additional vessels, all with a part to play to ensure the overall success of the operation. There were also land batteries raining down heavy artillery fire as well as bombers from the newly formed Royal Air Force, dropping incendiary devices on the German defensive positions.

Despite being hindered by an unexpected blanket of fog that had inconveniently laid itself across the Belgium coastline, the *Vindictive* eventually found the mouth of the canal it was looking for, careful not to be fooled by the possible repositioning of navigation buoys by the Germans. Confirming his position was correct, Commander Godsal turned the *Vindictive* straight towards the mouth of the canal and was immediately fired upon by German artillery batteries as well as nearby machine-gun positions. One of the German heavy guns had struck the ship's propeller, which prevented Godsal from being able to turn the *Vindictive* sideways into the mouth of the canal. Before the problem was realized Godsal was killed along with most of the other officers and men who were on the bridge at the time. With no one able to try and rectify the situation, the *Vindictive* drifted out of the canal and ran aground on a sandbank which resulted in her not fully blocking the entrance to the canal.

First Lieutenant Victor Crutchley, who was one of those wounded when the bridge was hit, understood the predicament he was in and that with the ship not manoeuvrable his only viable option was to order the ship to be scuttled where she was. Before he abandoned ship along with the rest of the crew, and with artillery shells and machine-gun fire raining down upon the *Vindictive*, he took a torch and searched for wounded men amongst the bodies of those lying on the deck of the stricken vessel. Only after he had satisfied himself that he would not be leaving behind any wounded comrades, did he make his way over the side and into the waiting motor launch ML254, which had managed to pick up thirty-eight members of the *Vindictive*'s crew.

Acts of bravery had been many during the raid, which was in keeping with the actions of those who had been on the raid at Zeebrugge, possibly none more so than those of Lieutenant Rowland Bourke, the commander of motor launch, ML276. On being informed that it was believed there were still men in the water near to where the *Vindictive* had been scuttled, he immediately headed towards it to look for survivors. Despite attracting heavy German

Rowland Richard Bourke, VC

machine-gun fire, Bourke and his crew returned to the *Vindictive* on a further four occasions before discovering Sir John Alleyne, the ship's navigation officer, who was badly wounded, along with two of the crew, who had all been clinging to the hull of an upturned boat. Having picked up the wounded sailors, Bourne began his dash for home, and safety. Almost immediately two German artillery shells struck ML276, the damage caused was not quite bad enough to render the craft inoperable, although it was sufficiently bad enough for her to have to be towed to safety by another motor launch. For his actions at Ostend, Bourke was awarded the Victoria Cross. He was one of the many who had also taken part in the raid on Zeebrugge on 23 April and for his actions that day he was awarded the Distinguished Service Order.

   Although he was born in London, he emigrated to Canada in 1902. After having been rejected by the Army, Navy and the Air Force, due to his poor eyesight, he returned to London at the outbreak of the war. He then successfully applied to join the Royal Naval Volunteer

*Dover Zeebrugge Raid, HMS **Vindictive***

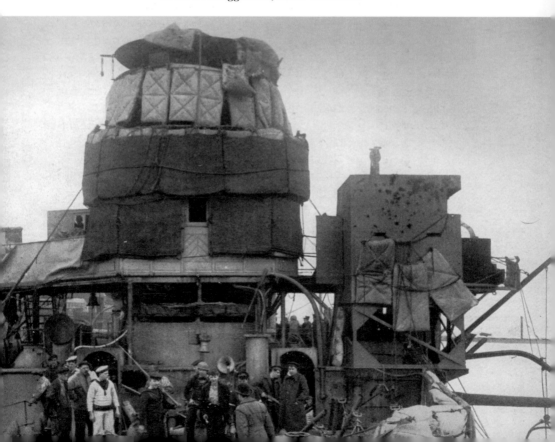

Reserve, where he served on motor launches. He was one of many who volunteered to take part in the Zeebrugge raid, but because of his poor eyesight his application to be involved was initially declined. His persistence to be allowed to take part in the Ostend raid eventually paid off.

It was not just the naval vessels that were involved in the actual raid that were damaged. Admiral Keyes' flag ship, HMS *Warwick*, struck a mine and was badly damaged although, along with the other surviving British naval vessels from the raid, she finally made her way back to Dover Harbour, arriving there the following morning.

British casualties from the raid were reported as being eight men dead, ten who were missing and a further twenty-nine who were wounded, compared with the German casualties of three killed and eight wounded.

Historically there will always be a debate as to the need and the effectiveness of the raids on Zeebrugge and Ostend by the Royal Navy. The reality was that neither of the attacks hindered German naval operations to any great degree. The Hindenburg Line had already been breached and, with the Allies already beginning to gain the upper hand on the Western Front, the timing of the attacks did not appear to be part of an overall military strategy aimed at bringing a speedier end to the war.

From the very outbreak of the war the belief among certain senior politicians and high ranking military personnel was that Germany would carry out a full scale invasion of Great Britain. Thankfully it never happened. How this belief ever came about is not known. It could have just as easily been somebody's gut feeling or a piece of military intelligence, either way it was a 'threat' that was taken very seriously, so much so that large numbers of British troops were kept along the east coast of England, just in case. These were undoubtedly difficult times as nearly all able bodied fit young men had already gone off to fight and more and more were needed as the war continued, so to keep so many back, just in case there was an invasion, showed just how seriously the threat was taken.

Late on in the war there was still real concern that the Germans might decide to invade Great Britain, and with Dover's position on the Kent coastline the town was an obvious location for them to try and land. With this possibility in mind, the Mayor of Dover issued the following notice:

Borough of Dover

'The emergency committee have received directions to issue the following instructions for the civil population in the event of a landing by the enemy in this country, an event less probable now than earlier in the war.

It has come to the notice of the Military Authorities that there is some doubt on the part of the civil population, particularly in the Eastern and South Eastern Counties, as to the preparations which have been made for the conduct and movement of the civil population in case of invasion or other emergency.

In order to allay any apprehension on this point, it is notified that complete schemes for regulating the action of the inhabitants have been framed by the central organising committee under the Lord Lieutenant of the County, but that it is not proposed to publish these in detail until an emergency actually exists.

Meanwhile, however, it is considered that the following instructions may be of service in giving the civil population a general outline of the course of action on their part which will be most helpful in enabling the authorities, both civil and military, to put their plans in to execution.'

The rest of the order was split into three sections under the headings of 'People', 'Transport' and 'Tools'.

Transport: in essence any kind of transport, whether it was mechanical, animal or a bicycle had to be handed in to the authorities if and when required to do so. If it was not possible to move a vehicle or animal to a designated location, then they could by military order be rendered unserviceable or destroyed, which in the case of an animal meant being killed.

Tools: any kind of tool was to be handed in at a pre-arranged location for either military use or disposal, along with all able bodied men, prepared and ready to carry out work as required of them by the military authorities.

People: this was more about ensuring that military personnel and transport had free and unhindered use of the transport system either by road or train. Only military personnel would be allowed to use the railways and civilians were advised to stay indoors unless ordered to do otherwise by military personnel.

Because of this prevailing threat and Dover's geographical location, it was decided that the town would form its own Local Emergency Committee. Not only were troops needed to defend the town in the case of an invasion, but the civilian population would also need to be evacuated to get them away from the fighting and out of harm's way. This would need to be carried out expediently and proficiently, so as to prevent loss of life. The Committee consisted of twelve men, one of whom was the Mayor and another the Chief Constable.

Early on in the war the Home Office had set out regulations for local authorities to inform their communities regarding what course of action needed to be taken in relation to the civilian population once it had become apparent that an invasion by German troops was imminent. Local authorities dealt with this instruction differently. The approach by Dover was a balanced one. On the one hand they considered the need to inform local residents of what was required of them if the need should arise to evacuate them to safety, but they balanced this need against the possibility of causing unnecessary panic, should they choose to do so. In the end Dover's Local Emergency Committee decided against passing on the Home Office's instructions in relation to evacuation procedures.

There was, however, a certain irony attached to this decision, as very early on in the war after the Allied defeat at, and subsequent retreat from Mons, there was a real concern that the Germans would not stop when they reached the sea, but instead would carry on across the Channel and invade Great Britain. With that possibility in mind the military authorities issued the following typed notice to every household in Dover, in October 1914:

Notice

THE INHABITANTS OF DOVER ARE INFORMED THAT UNDER MILITARY ORDERS THEY ARE TO EVACUATE THE TOWN IMMEDIATELY
    ALL CIVILIANS RESIDENT IN THE DISTRICT DESCRIBED

ON THE ENCLOSED SHEET MUST MEET AT THE PLACE OF ASSEMBLY AT

AND THERE AWAIT ORDERS TO LEAVE FOR THE COUNTRY ON FOOT. VEHICLES WILL, AS FAR AS POSSIBLE BE PROVIDED FOR THOSE UNABLE TO WALK. EACH PERSON MUST CARRY WARM CLOTHING AND FOOD AND DRINK FOR TWELVE HOURS. MR A C LENEY WILL ACT AS EVACUATING OFFICER WITH HEADQUARTERS AT THE TOWN HALL.

Evacuating a town the size of Dover would have been no easy task. The logistics of getting everybody together in one particular area at the same time would not have been easy for a start. There would have been the situation of having an extremely large group of people of all different ages, some who were not very mobile and some who were simply just not mobile at all. Babies and young children, pregnant women, hospital patients and the sick. Some would need transport to move them, how do you get such a large group to move along at the same pace, and what happens if the weather is bad, and it's raining, or snowing and cold. Not a situation that bears thinking about!

CHAPTER SEVEN

Dover Air Raids

Dover was a major port, in both a civilian and military sense, before the outbreak of the war in much the same way as Southampton, Folkestone, Portsmouth and Chatham were. Dover was deemed by the Germans to be a sufficiently important target that they carried out a total of 113 aerial attacks on it during the First World War, dropping a total of 185 bombs on Dover and its surrounding areas, killing twenty-three people, included three children. Seventy-one people were injured, including twelve children. Civilians or soldiers were killed on at least nine of these raids.

The first raid took place on the morning of Christmas Eve 1914 with the last one on the evening of 24 August 1918. The one raid that took place during 1914 was a significant one, because the bomb that was dropped was also the first one to land on British soil during the First World War. The following year, 1915, saw another two air raids targeting the town. There was a massive spike the following year with thirty-five raids taking place, but 1917 was the worst year of the war, with a further fifty-four raids, equating to roughly one a week. The worst month was September when thirteen raids took place. The final year of the war saw twenty-one German raids carried out over Dover, with the last one taking place on the evening of 24 August 1918, just eleven weeks before the end of the war.

The map shows in exact detail where each one of the bombs that were dropped on Dover, fell. Despite the large number of bombs that were dropped on the town, it can quite clearly be seen that more than fifty of them either landed in open fields or in the sea.

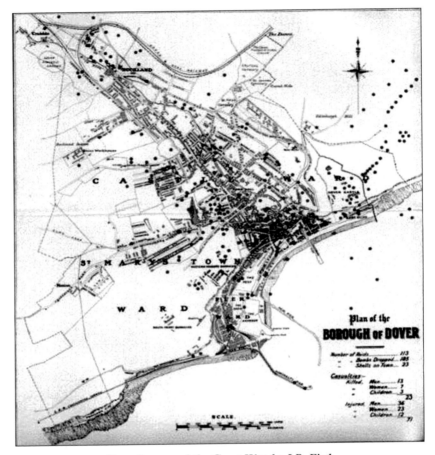

From **Dover and the Great War** *by J.B. Firth*

The caves at the Oil Mills in Snargate Street, which had originally been carved out of the solid chalk cliffs, were also used as an air raid shelter as were the six cells and the assortment of adjoining offices at Dover Police station.

The people of Dover were fortunate enough to have numerous air raid shelters in the event of the air raid siren being activated. There was the tunnel in Western Heights, the caves in Trevanion Street, the crypt underneath the Town Hall which could hold up to 800 people and the

Phoenix Brewery cellars in Castle Street during an air raid

cellars at the Phoenix Brewery in Castle Street which could hold up to 1,000 people.

Notice the woman on the far left of the picture, holding her much loved dog and the children in the front row who have blinked and closed their eyes as the flash of the camera has gone off.

Messrs Leney, who owned the Brewery, also provided their spare trucks and lorries for use by the Admiralty for the Naval Brigade, free of charge for the duration of the war.

The effectiveness of the strategy of German aerial bombing of the British mainland is questionable. It could be argued that it was an absolute waste of time, money, effort, machines as well as the lives of their men who were killed whilst carrying out these raids. In a military sense the raids actually had very little effect, as they did not cause any long term damage or destruction to any major British military establishment during the entire war. What they did do though was bring the war direct to the people of the British Isles. No longer was it just a war somewhere the other side of the English Channel and further afield, now it was something very real which the people of Dover were witnessing at first hand.

What these raids did achieve was to cause widespread alarm amongst the civilian population and uncertainty of when and where the next attack was going to be. Most of the attacks appeared to be somewhat random and more often than not fell within civilian populated areas rather than on military establishments, or indeed industrial areas which were carrying out work of a military nature.

CHAPTER EIGHT

Dover Patrol

Admiral Sir Reginald Bacon DSO, (second left)
Commander Dover Patrol 1915–17

Although the Dover Patrol was in place throughout the war, it is included in this chapter as they were still as proactive in the last year of the war as they were in the first. Historically their reputation for bravery and their steely determination to get the job done was greatly enhanced by the Zeebrugge and Ostend raids in April and May 1918.

Before the beginning of the First World War, Dover had been one of the major ports on the south coast of England and was a gateway of travel to Europe and beyond. All of that came to an abrupt end on 4 August 1914 when passenger ships and private individuals were replaced by military vessels, troops and supplies. But the town was to play an even bigger part in the war, in the shape of what became known as the Dover Patrol.

Dover became the home base for a Royal Navy command tasked with escorting hospital ships that brought wounded men back from France and Belgium, as well troop ships taking newly-trained soldiers to fight on the Western Front, trawler fleets that were catching fish for consumption on the home front and merchant vessels from around the world bringing in food stuffs and other essential items. As if this wasn't enough to contend with there were other routes across the English Channel which meant even more ships that had to be protected. Troop transporters regularly crossed between Folkestone and Boulogne, Southampton and Le Havre as well as the secret port at Richborough which had a route across the Channel to Dunkirk, where it delivered much needed supplies and equipment, such as horses, ammunition, fuel, tanks and rations. The port was run by the Inland Waterways Department of the Royal Engineers. The Dover Patrol had another base on the French side of the English Channel, at Dunkirk.

The vessels of the Dover Patrol were also tasked with mine laying as well as sweeping for enemy mines. They also had the unenviable job of keeping the English Channel safe from the German Navy, particularly the threat posed by their submarines. The Patrol was not just a group of up to date naval warships, it included aeroplanes and airships as well as trawlers, yachts, motor launches, and drifters which the Admiralty had seen fit to requisition, some of which they armed. Nor was it just the vessels which the Admiralty needed, it was the men who crewed them. They became part of the Royal Naval Volunteer Reserve.

Rear Admiral Hood had begun the First World War off the coast of Belgium with a small flotilla of Humber-class monitors that had been tasked with assisting Belgian land forces by bombing German positions during the Battle of Antwerp.

In March 1915 Hood was put in command of the Dover Patrol. He had been sent to Dover to amass a force that could safeguard the English Channel and the vessels who used it, put together from a rag tag selection of obsolete ships, some of which were so old, they were no longer on the Navy's active service list. When it was discovered that vessels of the Imperial German Navy were still managing to break through the defensive systems Hood had put in place, he was removed by Winston Churchill and put in charge of Force E, which consisted of cruisers and boarding vessels, operating in the waters off the south west of Ireland, directing and protecting arriving merchant vessels from attack.

Hood was later killed during the Battle of Jutland when his battlecruiser, HMS *Invincible*, was struck by a shell fired from the German vessel *Defflinger* which caused one of her magazines to explode with such force that she was literally blown in half. Only six members of the crew survived. Hood was one of the 1,021 members of *Invincible*'s crew who lost their lives that fateful day. His body was never recovered.

Admiral Sir Reginald Bacon became Commander of the Dover Patrol in 1915, a position he held until 1917, when he was succeeded by Admiral Sir Roger Keyes. During his time in charge attempts had been made to confine the German Navy, and in particular her submarines, to the North Sea, which restricted their effectiveness and made them easier to track.

In a joint operation, a North Sea mine barrage had been put in place by the Americans and the British, which consisted of more than 70,000 mines laid in a grid of eighteen lines that stretched from the Orkney Islands, across to the coast of Norway. There was a similar barrier in place at the northern end of the Dover straits, which was also designed to prevent German submarines from reaching the Atlantic. Despite its supposed effectiveness as a deterrent, British Naval Intelligence had received reports that U-boats were managing to break through the barriers under the cover of darkness. Bacon had repeatedly refused to illuminate the barrier during the hours of darkness. He was eventually ordered to do so by the First Sea Lord, Rosslyn Wemyss. The very next night a German submarine was discovered whilst attempting to breach the barrage and destroyed. He was replaced soon after by Sir Roger Keyes.

Although Keyes was born in the Punjab, India and died in Tingewick, in Buckinghamshire in 1945, aged seventy-three, he was actually buried in St James Cemetery, Dover, where a number of his colleagues from the Dover Patrol are also buried.

Protecting the English Channel was always going to be a difficult task, no matter who was in charge. It was undoubtedly one of the most important of the war from a British perspective, but there were different aspects to it. Besides the convoys they protected, the patrol had to search out German shipping and submarines, whilst at the same time preventing them from carrying out surprise attacks along the Kent coastline. They had to look out for mines that had been laid as well as try to prevent German Zeppelins and Gotha aircraft from attacking Dover and nearby stretches of the Kent coastline and making it further inland towards London.

The Dover Patrol had to succeed on every single occasion to be totally successful, but in fairness to them that was never going to be a realistic proposition. There was no radar to protect the coastline and pinpoint enemy attacks either by air or by sea. It was down to visual sightings and recognition of enemy aircraft and vessels.

To highlight how big a task it was for the Dover Patrol and just what a truly remarkable job they achieved, here are some facts and figures taken from the book by J.B. Firth, *Dover and the Great War*, which was published in 1919.

Between 5 August 1914 and 11 November 1918 there were 11,938 journeys that left Dover Harbour bound for France – an average of seven for every day of the war. This included 3,875 journeys by hospital ships and ambulance transports.

During the same period there were another 10,636 journeys that left from, and arrived at nearby Folkestone. In the main these ships were carrying troops, an estimated 8,124,858. That is an absolutely staggering amount of men who depended for their safety on the Dover Patrol. They also transported 14,050,461 items of mail, 3,690 vehicles, 373 motor cycles, 349 horses and 94,726 tons of stores.

A total of 125,100 merchant ships travelled through or across the English Channel during the war. Only sixty-three didn't make it. Of these it is known that forty-seven were sunk by mines, thirteen by torpedoes, one by German bombs, one by gunfire and one was torpedoed by an aircraft.

Between July 1915 and October 1918, English minesweepers

managed to destroy a total of 1,507 mines which had been laid by the Germans, with the French destroying a further 427.

All of this outstanding work came at a price. During the war, 295 officers and men, who were working on board trawlers engaged in mine sweeping, lost their lives, along with a further 256 who were working as part of the Drifter Patrol. The mine sweepers covered an area of more than 600 miles of sea each day.

At the then secret Port of Richborough, 10,000 steel barges loaded with 1,250,000 gross tonnage of equipment, including 650,000 tons of ammunition and 11,000 guns, crossed the Channel under the protection of the Dover Patrol. Not one barge was lost.

Sadly though, very little positive news was reported at the time, which was understandable in the circumstances, after all there was a war going on and the authorities had to consider public morale, which would not remain very high if they continually read about how successful the Germans were being at sinking Allied vessels and

Sir Roger Keyes

killing large numbers of civilians and naval personnel. Attacks on British soil from the air either from Zeppelin or Gotha aircraft raids, however, were not easy for the authorities to suppress.

The Dover Patrol was a much-needed service by the British and their Allies if they wanted to keep control of the open seas. By the end of 1917 German U-boats were accounting for 400 Allied ships each month. That was an absolutely astounding number of vessels to lose with such regularity. Each loss was sorely felt back in the UK. The goods lost, especially the food, were hard to replace expeditiously. Their loss started to have an impact which led eventually to the rationing of everyday food supplies throughout Britain, a system brought in by the government of the day who began to believe that if something was not done to curtail the continued heavy losses at sea, they could end up being starved out of the war, rather than losing it on the battlefields of the Western Front.

Although Britain and America had managed to greatly reduce the number of German U-boats reaching the Atlantic, some were still managing to breach the defensive netting that was in place at the northern end of the Dover Straits.

One of the sections of the Dover Patrol which is often forgotten was the air force, which included both the Royal Naval Air Service and the Royal Air Force, which acted independently of each other. To begin with the use of the Royal Air Force and prior to that the Royal Flying Corps, was dictated by the War Office, whilst the sea planes operating from the sea front, where the old skating rink used to be, was under the control of the Admiralty.

When Sir Roger Keyes, who had been in command of the Dover Patrol was subsequently presented with the Freedom of the Borough at Dover Town Hall, he sang the praises of the aircraft of the Dover Patrol and the part they played in the war in keeping Dover and London safe. He also highlighted the protection that they provided for shipping, both merchant and military, which sailed through and across the English Channel. Just their constant presence in the skies stopped an untold amount of Allied shipping from being sunk by German submarines, and the loss of possibly thousands of lives. By way of example, between 1 April 1918 and 31 October 1918 the Royal Air Force flew a total of 39,109 hours. They attacked 189 German submarines; they attacked 351 German aircraft, destroying 184 of them and damaging a further 151. They also managed to destroy thirty-two of the sixty-nine mines which they spotted as well. They dropped 15,313 bombs on enemy targets and flew a total of 3,441 convoy flights. Remember, these are not figures for the entire period of the war, but for just seven months.

CHAPTER NINE

Dover Volunteer Training Corps – 1914

With the outbreak of the war the town's territorial units were quickly mobilized and sent off to France, India and Mesopotamia, modern day Iraq. This left Dover void of any volunteer type of force, which was a concern. On 19 November 1914 there was a meeting at the Council Chamber which was chaired by the Mayor, Edwin Farley, at which Brigadier General Fiennes Henry Crampton, spoke. One of the topics discussed was the need for a local Volunteer Force, so that the town had some way of defending itself in the event of a German invasion. This was in line with what was taking place elsewhere across the country. At the time there were already one million men who had enlisted in their local Volunteer Training Corps. It gave these men, who were unable to enlist in the regular army, because of age, business commitments or infirmity, the ability to still do their bit for the war effort. By then Dover already had a Searchlight Corps.

A few days later a public meeting specifically to address the matter of the Volunteer Force, was held at the Town Hall. At this 305 men by agreed to join.

On 5 December 1914 the active work

Volunteer Training Corps meeting, 28 November 1914

of the Dover Volunteer Training Corps began when thirty men who would become the Corps instructors, began a trainers' course under the watchful eye of Sergeant Major Richards of the Cinque Ports Royal Engineers, at the Drill Hall in Liverpool Street. The course took place over a two-week period and meant the men having to give up each of their weekday evenings to pass.

During the same period, but for only four evenings of each of the two weeks, commencing on 8 December, 200 members of the newly formed corps, underwent a course of 'musketry instruction' at the Market Hall. The volunteers were taught how to use the army's service rifle of the time, the Lee Enfield .303. After the men had become suitably proficient in the handling of the weapon, they had to undergo a short course of miniature rifle firing in which they were required to reach a required standard before the Government Badge could be issued.

Mr George Jewell of 12 Effingham Crescent, Dover, wrote a letter to the editor of the *Dover Express*, which appeared in their Christmas Day edition.

'*Sir,*

I noticed by the local press that the much discussed subject of whether men of an age eligible for serving in the Forces, should be allowed to join the Corps or not has, so far, not been settled. Might I, Mr Editor, be permitted through your valued columns to suggest that the training of such a squad of men, i.e., between the ages of 19 and 38 years, would in no way be detrimental to the country.

If the corps is to be a combatant one, and there is any likelihood of the Germans landing a force, I maintain that every trained man will be required to defend the hearth and home. Of course, when the question of affiliating to the central body arises, then, and not until then, need the matter be further discussed. If headquarters refuses to enrol such men, I still consider that the training given will not be wasted, even if we only look at it from a disciplinary point of view. Why should the young men of Dover be deprived of being trained and making themselves fit to take up arms, if necessity arises? I, therefore, suggest that my proposition may be considered by the organisers of the Corps, instead of waiting indefinitely for a ruling from the central body, and probably keeping hundreds of men out of the Corps, in which case the Corps will not prove to be so useful as it was at first expected.

I remain yours faithfully
George Jewell.'

On the morning of Christmas Eve 1914 the Vice Lieutenant of Kent issued a notice to the entire civilian population of Kent. In it he advised all men that were able, to join either the Regular or Territorial Forces. Those who were unable to do so were advised to join the Dover Volunteer Training Corps. The notice, which had been handed out, included an enrolment form for the Corps, and information that the first parade of the newly formed unit was to take place at the Liverpool Street Drill Hall.

Anyone who refused to join the Dover VTC may, under the orders issued, be instructed by a Special Constable to carry out non-combatant duties. In order to be recognised as a 'combatant' a member of the public had to be a member of a volunteer corps which had been affiliated to the Central Association of Volunteer Training Corps. Only members of such corps would receive the official badge that had been issued by the British Government to combatants. This was an extremely important point for the public to grasp, because if they weren't a member of such a corps, and they fired upon a German soldier in the case of an enemy invasion, if captured they were liable to be shot as they would not have any of the protections afforded to a captured soldier, and would be treated as a 'freedom fighter' or a member of the 'resistance'.

Another notice for the public's consumption was issued by the Police in Dover, which allowed for the town's Special Constables to enrol in the Volunteer Training Corps.

'Special Constables are to be allowed to join volunteer corps for the purposes of drill. In the first place they must remember they are special constables, and, as such must hold themselves available at a moment's notice for any call that may be made upon them by the Police or emergency committees.'

The local authorities in Dover were keen to endorse the theme that all able bodied male 'Dovorians' should, at the earliest opportunity, 'join whatever force they are eligible for'. There appeared to be a, 'we're all in it together' attitude within Dover in relation to the war. Whether that was how the people of the town actually felt or whether it was a theme being pushed by the local authorities, isn't clear.

At 7pm on Saturday, 2 January 1915, the first parade and enrolment meeting of the Dover VTC took place. It was now time for the talking to stop and the idea to become a reality and the men who had intimated that they wanted to become part of the Corps to sign up to do their bit for their community in the case of a German invasion. Every effort had been made to provide men with the chance to sign up for the Corps, with numerous locations around the town providing enrolment notices well in advance of the meeting on 2 January. The Corps was only open to men who were not of military age.

At the same meeting, Sergeant Major Richards of the Royal Engineers was provided with a purse containing £5 as a late 'Christmas Box' which had been collected among the men whom he was training for the Corps. The gift came as a total surprise but was very much appreciated by him.

In the edition of the *Dover Express* dated 8 January 1915, was a piece about the Volunteer Training Corps both at a national as well as a local level. The last paragraph appeared to endorse the theme of men 'doing their bit' for the war effort on the home front by enrolling in the Dover VTC, by employing the tactic of embarrassment. See what you think.

The Future Question

Ten years hence when your children ask you what you remember about the Great War of 1914-15 and you describe as best you can what occurred, they are sure to finish up with the question: "And what were you doing?" Surely the answer is not to be, "I did nothing," but rather, "Well, I was not of military age but I did the best I could, I joined the Dover Volunteer Training Corps."'

The reference to the 'Great War of 1914-15' highlights the belief by some, and clearly a view held by elements of the Press, that the war was not going be a long one.

By February 1915 a total of 302 men had enlisted and were formed into two companies, and so it was that the Dover VTC was officially launched. The men continued to undergo regular instruction which in the main focused on 'Musketry' and Infantry drill, but there was still a desire to obtain even more recruits.

On Saturday, 2 February 1915 a meeting of the Corps took place at the Riding School in Liverpool Street. About 200 members attended.

At the time there were several young men who were members of the Dover VTC, but who were still too young to enlist in the Army. They hadn't joined the Corps to escape having to join the Army, no, it was more a case of providing themselves with the best preparation for when the time came for them to do so. Already knowing how to carry out drill and use a rifle, would have been a big advantage for them.

At the other end of the age range there were men in the Corps who were over 38 years of age, too old to join the Army, as the age limit was at that time, but who still wanted to do their bit, with an upper age of 60. Some were retired soldiers and many had no military experience whatsoever, but all of them had come together in a common cause at a time when their country needed them. This situation simply mirrored men who were serving in the Army. Some were professional soldiers, whilst others were labourers, miners, carpenters, butchers, policemen or postmen, but because a war had come along in their lifetime, they joined up, each of them feeling that it was the right thing to do.

What separated members of the Corps from their counterparts in the Regular Army and the Territorials, was that they were volunteers in the truest sense of the word. They did not receive any pay for what they did. Once having enrolled in the Corps, they were expected, not obliged, to attend at least forty drills and remain a member for the duration of the war. Unlike members of the armed forces who had to be attested and swear allegiance to the King, men who joined the Corps, did not have the same requirement placed upon them.

With the outbreak of war came a desire from men of all ages, not just young men, swept along on a wave of national pride and fervour, to want to do their duty for their king, their country, their family and themselves. For some the only option which they had was to join the Volunteer Training Corps.

On 24 February 1915 the Corps had a parade and march for the first time, with 220 members in attendance. With their Commandant,

Sir William Crundall, a local timber merchant who lived at Woodside River in the town, leading them, they left the Drill Hall in Liverpool Street and took a route through the town's main street as far as Tower Hamlets, and then returned to the Drill Hall via Maison Dieu Road with the band of the East Surrey Regiment.

By now the Corps had selected its officers. They were:

Mr A.C. Leney and Mr T. Basil Duguid – Corps rank, company commanders, which had an equivalent Army rank of major.

Mr J. Wood and Mr P. Hodgson – Corps rank, second in command of company, which had an equivalent Army rank of captain.

Mr C. Flashman, Dr Kent, Mr A. Wright, Mr F. Crundall, Mr Vernon Shone, Dr Pinhorn and Mr A.M. Evanson – Corps rank of platoon commander, which had an equivalent Army rank of lieutenant or second lieutenants.

Mr Rutley Mowell – Corps rank of adjutant, which was exactly the same in the Army.

Mr O.G.B. Jones was the assistant adjutant and musketry instructor.

Mr W.T. Barron – Corps rank of quartermaster, which was exactly the same in the Army.

Mr R. Panter – Corps rank of regimental quartermaster sergeant, which was exactly the same in the Army.

Mr Garland, Mr Nicholls, Mr Browne, Mr Mant, Mr Summers, and Mr Toms – Corps rank of platoon sergeant, which was exactly the same as in the Army.

On 23 April 1915, the Mayor of Dover, Mr Farley had a letter of appeal published in support of the Dover VTC.

'Dear Sir,

Will you allow me to appeal to your readers for support in reference to the Dover Volunteer Training Corps. This Corps which has been established with the sanction of the War Office and with the active approval of General Crampton, consists of men and youths not of military age who have banded themselves together for the defence of their homes in this time of national need.

The men receive no payment whatever for their services and the burden of putting themselves in uniforms and providing themselves with equipment and arms falls entirely upon the

Corps, as no funds are provided by the National Exchequer for this purpose. There are nearly already 400 members of the Corps and it is estimated that the cost of arming, equipping and putting in to uniform will amount to not less than £6 a head. Many of the Corps consist of working men who already subscribed such sums as they are able towards the expenses of the Corps, but it is not fair to expect them in addition to giving their time to also be able to find the necessary funds for their equipment. I am therefore appealing to the inhabitants of Dover to assist in this movement which I believe is one calculated to produce a splendid spirit of patriotism, loyalty and self-sacrifice.

Whenever this country has been in time of great national need as at present, there have never been lacking men prepared to do their duty and I trust that the present generation in Dover will not be behind the splendid example set to them forefathers 100 years ago when there was formed from Dover and the district a body called the Cinque Ports Fencibles.'

Even with the war costing the British Government in excess of £5 million a week, it seemed somewhat strange that they were not prepared to fund a body of men, which they had officially endorsed and sanctioned nationwide, and who would be the last line of defence in the event of a German invasion.

CHAPTER TEN

Police and Special Constables

By the start of the First World War policing was still less than one hundred years old, the service conditions of which had not changed that much over time. Throughout England and Wales, Watch Committees were the local government bodies which were in charge of policing, with the power to appoint constables for their own areas. Although this process changed in some areas in 1889, Police forces that were within a single borough retained their Watch Committee.

Many Police officers who were in post at the outbreak of the war, had previously been soldiers or sailors, which meant that many of them were recalled to serve with the Colours. Although the role of Special Constables had been around since the time of the Norman Conquest in 1066, they really came in to their own during the First World War, with Police forces having to operate with fewer full time officers.

On 29 September 1914 at the monthly meeting of the Dover Town Council, the Watch Committee delivered a report covering the period July to September 1914, this including Police pay and pensions. The Chief Constable of Dover, Mr David Fox, presented his report for the same time period which covered, amongst other matters, the different offences that had been dealt with by his officers, as well as the number of officers who had reported sick, those who had subsequently returned to work and those who were still absent.

The Town Clerk submitted a letter which had been received from the Home Office regarding the steps to be taken for the continuous preservation of order during the war, by the strengthening of the regular Police force and the creation of a force of Special Constables.

The letter went on to add that the Government was prepared to make a contribution of one half of the pay of the extra men not exceeding fifty per cent above the authorized strength of the force on the terms named, but that all vacancies must be filled.

In response to the letter, the Chief Constable surprisingly stated that no vacancies had arisen as a result of any of his officers having been called up for war service, and that he did not consider it necessary at the time to increase the strength of the Force, especially as he had a list of fifty Special Constables who were willing to serve and who could be called upon at a moment's notice. He added that as from 2 October the force would have two vacancies, caused by the resignations of Sergeant Figg and Inspector Palmer. He said that his men had not been allowed to take any annual leave, but that they were permitted one rest day every two weeks.

The issue concerning whether or not to increase the number of Police constables in Dover from sixty-six to sixty-eight, caused some lively debate amongst those present, with some councillors claiming that the number of Police officers in Dover was already proportionately high for a town with a population of 40,000, compared to other towns in the district. Councillor Edward Chitty informed the meeting that he had previously been visited by His Majesty's Inspector of Constabulary, who had stated that he felt the vacancies in the Dover Police force should be filled and wanted to know why they hadn't been, and that in the absence of some definite and sufficient reason explaining why, he would not be able to report that the force had been efficiently maintained. At the time, the wage of a Police constable in Dover, was 32s per week or £80 a year.

After some lively debate on the matter, a vote was taken and it was decided not to increase the Police numbers in Dover from sixty-six to sixty-eight, even though both the Watch Committee and the Chief Constable had recommended in its favour.

A notice appeared in the *Dover Express* of 4 December 1914 advertising the appointment of two constables.

'Borough of Dover Police Force
The Watch Committee will receive applications for the appointment of two Constables on probationary duty for three months.

No person is eligible whose age is less than 21 or more than 25 years; nor unless he is in height 5 feet 9 inches at least; and can read and write.

Applications, in the handwriting of the applicant, on forms to be obtained at the Police Station, must be sent to me on or before Saturday, 12th December, accompanied by testimonials.

All applicants must present themselves to the Chief Constable previously, and attend at the Town Hall on Tuesday, 15th December, at 2.15pm.

Canvassing (either directly or indirectly) the members of the Watch Committee and of the Council is prohibited.

(By Order)

R.E. Knocker Town Clerk
Town Clerk's Office, 69 Castle Street, Dover,
27th November 1914.'

The Police often seem to be forgotten when it comes to addressing the efforts of organizations during the First World War. It could be argued that some Police officers, who worked in small village communities in nice rural parts of the country, didn't have it too bad. They would have had a relatively small area to cover and would have known most, if not all, of the people whom they policed, but working in a busy and densely populated large town, would have been a totally different experience.

At the outbreak of war Dover reportedly had a population of 40,000 people, whilst the 1911 Census shows the total as being 43,553. But it has to be remembered that from the early months of the war, with thousands of military personnel coming in to the town, that number would have been much larger. The number of full time Police officers in the Dover Borough Police at the beginning of the war was just sixty-six, with no more than two thirds of that number likely to have been on duty at any one time. Dover also had a list of approximately fifty Special Constables who were available to be called upon at a moment's notice.

The Chief Constable of Dover Borough Police was Mr David Henry Fox, who lived at 16 Effingham Crescent, Dover, with his wife, Susan, and their six children, Percy, Mildred, Frederick, Annie, Ernest and

Elsie. He had joined the local Police in 1881 aged 17, prior to which he had been employed as a hay cutter. By 1901 he was a sergeant and he became the Chief Constable of the Force in 1908. He died in Dover on 12 February 1924 aged 60, when the family home was at 16 Park Street in Dover. In his will he left £1,534 5 s 10d to his widow, Susan. This was the equivalent of four years' wages as a Chief Constable.

Chief Constable David Fox certainly did lead from the front, as reported in the *Dover Express* newspaper, dated 31 March 1916.

On the evening of Friday, 24 March Mr Fox was walking near his home in Effingham Crescent when he heard the sound of footsteps coming from behind him. Being 8.30pm it was quite dark, but he could see that three men had stopped outside Dr Long's motor garage. He then heard one of the men say, 'Cut the string', followed by a rustling of paper. Totally unperturbed, Mr Fox crossed over the road to approach the men, not having the slightest idea of what would confront him. He switched on his torch and the three men, who he could see by their uniforms were soldiers, started acting furtively, as they stood in a line up against a wall, whilst placing items under their coats. He looked down and saw some string on the pavement in front of them. Mr Fox was soon afterwards joined by Constable Duncan who had been on duty at the nearby Police station. Almost immediately one of the three men ran off. Mr Fox then arrested one of the men whose name was Donovan, whilst Police Constable Duncan arrested the other man, Youthed, before taking them back to the Police station where they were searched and found to be in possession of socks and clothes which had been stolen earlier that day from Mr Beer's outfitters shop at 80 Biggin Street, Dover.

At their subsequent trial, Donovan and Youthed, who were members of the Royal Fusiliers, having been transferred from the East Surrey Regiment, were both found guilty and sentenced to fourteen days hard labour.

In the three months between December 1916 and February 1917, twenty-two members of the National Union of Police and Prison Officers (NUPPO) were sacked for belonging to the union. As a side issue, those sacked from the Police then found themselves liable to be conscripted for military service.

Before the war was over Police officers in the United Kingdom would strike. This happened on 30 August 1918 when some 12,000 members of the Metropolitan Police came out on strike in support of Constable Tommy Theil who had been sacked for belonging to a union. The troubles between NUPPO, senior Police officers and the Government had been brewing for some time, but collectively, the Commissioner of the Metropolitan Police and the Home Secretary did not seem to have grasped the seriousness of the situation.

Frustrated by the authorities' lack of response, NUPPO made their demands, which were, a pay increase for all officers, a war bonus, pension rights to include a Policeman's widow, a shortening of the pension entitlement from thirty years to twenty-six years, an allowance for school age children and official recognition of their union. They gave fair warning that if their demands were not met in full by midnight on 29 August 1918, the Police officers of the Metropolitan Police in London would go on strike. The Commissioner of the Metropolitan Police, Sir Edward Henry, displaying arrogance of neolithic proportions, responded to this ultimatum by issuing an official Police order banning the union and promising instant dismissal to any of his officers who were discovered to be associated with it, believing that this would be an adequate deterrent in preventing any of his men from daring to strike. By being dismissed officers would also lose any pension rights they had acquired. The Government, in the shape of the Home Secretary, took a similar tough approach.

Having grossly underestimated the strength of feeling amongst rank and file Police officers and their desire for better pay and conditions, the Chief Constable was somewhat taken aback when, at midnight on 29 August 1918, 12,000 members of the Metropolitan Police walked out on strike. The Government was totally shocked and surprised with the immediate speed in which NUPPO carried out their threat, and the solidarity shown by their members. On the same day that the strike took place 1,115 British and Dominion military personnel were killed in the war.

Troops were deployed at prominent locations all over London, not only to keep the peace and to prevent stealing, looting and public disorder, but to send out a strong message to the general public that all was well and that it was business as usual.

At the time of the strike the Prime Minister, Lloyd George, was in France, meeting troops. He immediately returned to England and arranged a meeting with NUPPO's Executive Board, where he agreed to all their demands, except the last one asking for official recognition of the Police Union. Lloyd George's reply would later be seen as a delaying tactic, when he stated that he could not provide the recognition that the union had requested during a time of war.

What happened in London was followed with interest all around the country, not just by fellow Police officers, but also those who were empowered to employ them. Dover was no different. The extra demands placed on an undermanned Police force, whose constables were subject to a discipline system that was at best harsh. There was an unarguable expectation to work extremely long hours without any extra pay, as part of a wage structure which saw experienced officers earning less than unskilled labourers, this in turn left the door wide open to an environment of corruption.

Here is a list, as far as I have been able to establish, of the men who served in the Dover Borough Police Force in the years immediately before the outbreak of the war as well as the years 1914 –1918.

Constable Arthur Charles Fleet. He lived at 76 Oswald Street, Dover, although at the time of his death on 19 September 1959, at the Royal Victoria Hospital in Dover, he had moved to 140 Elms Vale Road in the town. He was survived by his widow, Annie Maria Fleet, to whom in his Will he left the princely sum of £1,924 19s 10d. This was a staggering sum of money for a constable whose wages would have been between £80 to £90 a year, making it the equivalent of more than twenty-three years' pay. This was £400 more than what the Chief Constable had left in his Will.

Constable John Edward Blaskett, lived at 5 Monroe Cottages, Manor Road, Maxton in Dover. He was a married man and was 27 years of age by the outbreak of the war. He was born and bred in Dover, worked there and in 1974, aged 87, he died there.

Constable Alexander Maxwell Bond, lived at 2 East Street, Dover. He was a married man with two young daughters.

Constable William Alexander Bowkley, lived at 28 Malmans Road, Dover.

Constable Ernest Albert Cadman, lived at 6 Clarendon Street,

Dover, which was his uncle and aunt's house. His brother George Sidney Cadman, served in the Navy as a cook during the war, having enlisted some eight years before the outbreak of hostilities on 8 May 1906. Having served for ten years on thirteen different ships, his last ship being, HMS *Cyclops*. He was placed on the Reserve list on 30 June 1916, which was surprising as the war was still going on at that time.

Constable William C. Court was a proud Scotsman who, having been born in 1866, was already 48 years of age by the beginning of the war. He was a married man living with his wife, Sophia, and their two children, William and Margaret, at 6 Oswald Street, Dover.

Constable George Andrew Duncan, lived with his wife, Lavinia and their two children, David and Clara, at 9 Beaconsfield Road, Dover. He was originally born in Roorkee, India in 1875.

Constable Ernest Edward Dunford, lived at 53 Oswald Road, Dover, with his wife, Ellen, and two young sons, John and Daniel.

Constable William Arthur Fagg, lived with his wife, Alice, and their five children at 103 Oswald Road, Dover.

Constable George Finch, lived with George and Margaret Robson at 6 Kingswood Villas, Crabble Avenue, Dover, as a boarder. When he died on 24 July 1938, he was living at Rose Cottage, Lower Road, River, near Dover, although he actually died at the New Inn Hotel at Maidstone.

Constable Horatio Norman Cecil Jack Fogg, lived at 8 Kingswood Villas, Crabble Avenue, Dover, with his wife, Helen, whom he married on 18 May 1887, with their two sons, Arthur and Norman and daughter, Ivy.

Constable Percy James Fox, lived at 28 Oswald Road, Dover, with his wife, Elizabeth and their two children, Gladys and Reginald. Percy, although just a plain old constable within the rank structure of the Police Force, was the son of the Chief Constable of Dover Borough Police, David Henry Fox. He was also the father of the Chief Constable's two grandchildren. Whether either role earned him any kind of privilege or favouritism in the eyes of the Chief Constable, is sadly not recorded.

Constable Frederick W. Hicks, lived at 52 Oswald Road, Dover, with his wife, Elizabeth, and daughter, Maude.

Constable George Albert Merricks, lived at 24 Charlton Avenue, Dover, with his wife, Edith, although by the time of his death on 25 June 1964, his home address was 10 Stanhope Road, Dover. In his Will he left the sum of £2,591 to Reginald Charles Merricks, who was either his son or brother, presumably as his wife had predeceased him.

Constable George Richards, lived at 30 Oswald Road, Dover, with his wife, Susan, and their two children, Harold and Winifred, which made them next door neighbours of Percy James Fox, the son of the Chief Constable. At the time of George's death in 1951, he and Susan were living at 15 De Burg Hill, Dover.

Constable John W.E. Smith lived at 17 Kimberley Terrace, Dover, with his wife Bessie, their son, also named John and daughter Queenie.

Constable George Spatcher, lived at 40 Lascelles, Dover with his wife, Jane and their two daughters, Dorothy and Grace.

Constable John Brown, lived at 25 Winchelsea Terrace, Dover, with his wife, Charlotte.

Constable Benjamin Ford Richard Brown, lived at 13 Crabble Hill Terrace, Dover, with his wife, Emmeline, and their two children, Bert and Queenie.

Constable Frank Hanford, lived at 30 Liverpool Street, Dover, which was the home of John and Emmeline Woodward. The entry for him on ancestry.co.uk, says he was a constable with the Metropolitan Police. I wondered whether it should be Dover Police, as in the days of the First World War, Police officers were stationed in the towns where they lived and were in effect part of the community; even when they were off duty they could still be called upon at a moment's notice, and quite often were.

Constable Alexander Kerr, lived at Clifton House, Frith Road, Barton Road, Dover, with his wife Alice, and their three children, Maud, William, and Marion.

Constable Henry Thomas Leeming, lived at 5 Old Park House, Dover, with his wife Ellen, and their two daughters Helen and

Gwendoline. He died at the Royal Victoria Hospital in Dover on 15 November 1959.

Constable Charles Morecroft, lived at 43 Winchelsea Street, Dover, with his wife, Mabel, and their two sons, Charles and Albert.

Constable James Riches, lived at Isca Cottage, Crabble Hill, Dover, with his wife, Annie, and their three children, Harold, Lulu and Albert.

Constable Walter William Spinner, lived at 6 Crabble Hill, Dover, with his wife, Maria, and their five children, Alfred, Walter, Louise, Elsie and Rose.

Constable William Vernon Taylor, lived at 17 Winchelsea Terrace, Dover, with his wife, Alice, and their young son, Bernard.

Constable Albert Baker, lived at 45 Longfield Road, Dover, with his wife Fanny, and their three children, Gilbert, Dorothea and baby Albert.

Constable George Edward Hodges, lived at 27 Longfield Road, Dover, with his wife Agnes, and their two daughters, Helen and Ethel. When George, an only child, was a boy growing up, his father Henry, was a farm bailiff by trade, which was profitable enough for him to be able to employ two servants.

Constable George Noel, lived at 31 Longfield Road, Dover, with his wife, Eliza, and their two sons, Bertrand and George.

Constable Arthur H. Overdun lived at 14 De Burg Street, Dover, with his wife, Gertrude, and their two sons, Arthur and Cecil.

Constable Albert Petley, lived at 1 Thrift Cottages, Shooters Hill, Buckland, Dover, with his mother Eliza and sister, Rhoda.

Constable William Ratcliffe, lived at 57 Pioneer Road, Crabble Hill, Dover, with two brothers, Francis and Horace, as well as his two sisters, Gertrude and Ethel.

Constable Henry Edwin Roberts, lived at 62 Longfield Road, Dover, with his wife Annie and his mother-in-law, Elizabeth Anne Pierce.

Constable Mark Taylor, lived at 109 Heathfield Avenue, Buckland, Dover, with his wife, Helen, and a male lodger, Ernest Albert Gower, who was a clerk in a wholesale grocers. On 23 June 1915, when he was 43 years of age, Mark enlisted in the Army Service Corps at Dover as a Driver (108259) with the 2nd Advanced Horse Transport Depot.

He had previous military experience, having served with the local volunteer Royal Garrison Artillery, before the war years. He left for France on 13 August 1915 not returning to England until 19 January 1918. He was finally demobbed on 21 February 1919, when he then re-joined Dover Borough Police and continued his career.

Constable Arthur G. Turner, lived at 24 Pioneer Road, Crabble Hill, Dover, with his mother, Jane Turner, and his four sons, Ethelbert, Arthur, Alexander and Ernest. The British Army medal rolls index for the First World War, shows an Arthur G. Turner who first arrived in France on 17 January 1915, on board the SS *Willow Branch*, where he served with the East Kent Regiment as Private 2/5257 before transferring to the Labour Corps as Private 443874. He may possibly be the same man.

Constable James Herbert Kines, lived at 14 Vale View Road, Dover, with his wife Sarah.

Constable John Cooney, lived at 65 Buckland Avenue, Dover, with his wife, Ada, and their children George, Elizabeth and Harriet.

Constable William Crawford, lived at 24 Elm Vale Road, Dover, with his wife, Eliza, and their adopted son, Vivian. William and Eliza had married in 1895 and had no children of their own. William is shown as being with the 'Metro' Police, so I am not certain if he was in fact a member of the Dover Borough Police. It was not usual for a man to be a Policeman in the town that he did not live in. It has been suggested that the Met had a Special Branch unit in Dover of which these 'Metro' Police may have been a part.

Constable John Henry Groombridge, lived at No.1 Upper Lodge Lane, with his wife Emily.

Constable William Pierce, lived at 12 Wood Street, Dover, with his wife Gertrude and their daughter May.

Constable Albert Edward Smithen, lived at 13a Queen Street, Dover, with his wife Elizabeth.

Constable Walter Henry Southey, lived at the Fire Station in Queen Street, Dover, with his wife Lizzie, his daughters Dorothy, Daisy and Lizzie, along with their son, Edward.

Constable Thomas Henry Beer, lived at 18 Markland Road, Dover, with his wife Anne, and their daughter, Joyce.

Constable Sydney Booth, lived at 57 Balfour Road, Dover, with his wife Mary, and their son Sydney junior.

Constable Charles Ernest Dane, lived at 53 Church Road, Dover, with his wife Jessie, their son Stuart, their daughter Ada and his mother, Eleanor Dane. At the time of his death, the family home was at 5 Kitchener Road in Dover.

Constable William Gibson, lived at 51 Easton Road, Dover, with his wife Blanch, and their daughter Gwendoline.

Constable George Greenland, lived at 1 Chiltern Gardens, Dover, along with his wife, Elizabeth, and their children William and Winifred.

Constable William Edwin Hurk, lived at Ivydene, St Radigunds Road, Dover, with his wife Anne, and their niece, Gertrude.

Constable Lewis Arthur Blackman, lived at 79 South Road, Lower Hamlet, Dover, with his wife, Anne, their children Sidney, Albert, Charles and Rose. Lewis's elder son, Sidney, had been a printer before the war, but he enlisted on 25 October 1915 aged 19, as a Private (72465) in the Royal Army Medical Corps and became part of the 18th Field Ambulance. He arrived in France on 25 September 1916, where he remained until 18 May 1919. Sidney was a fortunate young man. One of the Army's discipline offences was for 'leaving a post without orders'. This offence was deemed to be so serious, that it was punishable by death. His Army service record shows that on 10 October 1918, he was disciplined for 'leaving his post whilst on guard in the field'. His punishment was to 'forfeit 7 days' pay'.

Constable Frederick Kingsmill, lived at 4 Washington Villas, Monins Road, Dover, with his wife, Sarah, and their three children, Florence, Lydia and Leslie.

Constable Ernest Kingsmill, was six years younger than his brother Frederick, but like him, he had become a Policeman working for the Dover Borough Police. He lived at 13 Kitchener Road in Dover, with his wife Annie, and their children Frederick and Clara.

Constable George Lawrence, lived at 3 Washington Villas, Monins

Road, Dartford, with his wife Emmeline, and their children George, Mildred and William.

Constable William J. Popple, lived at 4 Down Cottages, Lower Road, River, Dover, with his wife, Florence, and their children Florence and William.

Constable Frederick Pott, lived at 10 Alexander Place, Buckland, London Road, Dover, which was his parent's home, along with his two brothers, Edwin and Alfred, and sister Mary. Edwin had enlisted as a Private (142) in the 4th Battalion, The Buffs, at Dover on 14 April 1908, at the age of 26, but prior to this he had already been a member of the 1st Volunteer Battalion, The Buffs (East Kent Regiment), between 14 November 1902 and 13 April 1908. He arrived in India on 29 October 1914 where he stayed until 4 August 1915. From there he was sent to Aden where he remained until 4 February 1916. He went on to India and whilst there he was promoted to the rank of sergeant. He remained there until 28 October 1919 before enduring a three week journey sailing back to England arriving on 19 November 1919. He was finally demobbed on 16 January 1920 having served with the British Army for more than eleven years. After his return, he moved to 29 Mayfield Avenue, Dover.

Constable Alfred Charles Starford, lived at 30 Kitchener Road, Dover, with his wife Elizabeth.

Inspector Frederick Richard Palmer, lived at 101 Buckland Avenue, Dover, with his wife Ellen, and their four sons, Bernard, Lewis, William and Harry.

Constable Robert Charles Vincent, lived at 21 Church Road, Maxton, Dover, with his wife Ellen.

Constable Horace Kemp, lived at 12 Elms Vale Road, Dover, with his mother, Ellen Kemp.

Sergeant Daniel Moore, lived at 9 St Johns Road, Folkestone Road, Dover, with his wife Frances, and their daughter Queenie.

Sergeant Edward M. Fox, was a widower who lived at 17 Woods Place, Dover, with his four children, Alfred, Margaret, Reginald and Annie. Alfred, the eldest, served during the First World War as a private (1419) with the 4th Battalion, The Buffs, which was a Territorial Unit. He initially enlisted for four years at the age of only 17 on 12 April

1908 at Dover, prior to which he had been a telegram boy for the Post Office. Once he had completed his four years' service he then enlisted as a private (200130) in the 1st/4th Battalion of the same regiment, on 12 April 1912, but interestingly enough his Army service record also records him as still being 17 years of age. He was initially sent to India arriving on 29 October 1915 where he remained until 4 August 1915. From there he went to Aden before returning to India on 5 February 1916 where he remained for the rest of the war, leaving Bombay on 24 October 1919 on board the SS *Nevassa* bound for Southampton. He ending up in the rank of Sergeant, and was finally demobbed, signing off at the Crystal Palace Dispersal Unit on 8 November 1919, nearly a year after the war had ended, by which time the family home was at 2 Elms Vale Road, Dover.

Sergeant Harry John Hambrook, lived at 54 Oswald Road, Dover with his wife Alice, and their three children, Eleanor, Henry, who before the war was a conductor on the trams, and Elsie. Henry enlisted in the Army aged 19 on 26 August 1914, with the war just three weeks old, joining the 102nd Anti-Aircraft Section of the Kent Royal Garrison Artillery as a gunner (121672). He also served with the 30th and the 120th Anti-Aircraft Sections. Before he had enlisted, Henry moved to 32 Balfour Road, Dover. He survived the war and was demobbed on 31 March 1919.

Detective Sergeant Frank Campany, lived at 42 Marine Parade, Dover with his wife Sarah. The couple had married in 1894.

Detective Sergeant Thomas McGrath, was a single man, who lodged at 4 Avenue Road, Dover, the home of Mr and Mrs Francis Carpenter. Thomas might have been a member of the Metropolitan Police, which is what it appears to suggest on the 1911 Census, but once again the ambiguity about living in Dover and working in London arises. He definitely wasn't a member of the Railway Police.

Constable Percy Harman, lived with his parents, George, who was a retired Policeman, and Mary Harman, at 5 Churchill Street, Dover, along with his brothers, Arthur, who was a tailor and Sidney who was a furniture clerk. Neither of them appear to have served in the military during the war. He also had a younger sister, Ethel.

Sergeant Henry Morris, lived at 1 Astley Avenue, Dover with his wife, Emma, and their two sons, Robert and Lambert. Lambert had enlisted in the 4th Battalion, The Buffs, two months before his nineteenth birthday, on 21 April 1909 at Dover, as Private 910505 and left having completed his four years of service on 17 January 1913. He re-enlisted on 1 September 1914, becoming Private 1524.

Other men who are known to have served in the Dover Borough Police during the First World War are as follows:

Sergeant Figg
Constable King
Sergeant Riley
Constable Loveridge
Constable Harvie
Inspector Scutt
Detective Sergeant Mount
Constable/Acting Sergeant Ovenden

There was an interesting article in the *Dover Express* on 4 December 1914. It concerned changes in the Dover Police Force due to the retirement of Police Inspector Scutt, after having served the town for twenty-seven years. In 1904 he sustained injuries to his legs whilst attending a fire, from which he never fully recovered. He was by all accounts, a highly respected member of the force.

On 5 January 1915 a special presentation was made to him at the quarterly parade of the Dover Borough Police by the Mayor, Councillor Farley. It was a handsome timepiece with the following inscription engraved on it: 'Presented to Inspector Charles S. Scutt by the members of the Dover Borough Police Force as a mark of their respect and esteem on his retirement after 27 years and six months service. 29th December 1914.'

The Chief Constable, Mr Fox, knew Inspector Scutt personally, having already been in the Dover Borough Police Force when the latter had joined. He had always known him to be conscientious in his work and an inspiration to his men and was sorry that he was retiring. There was even more praise from the Mayor who had been a childhood friend, and somebody whom he held in the highest esteem; making the presentation had given him a lot of personal pleasure. Mr Scutt was extremely grateful for the presentation, commenting that he took with him in to his retirement some very pleasant memories from his time working in the force.

Inspector Scutt was 47-year-old Charles Savage Scutt who lived with his wife, Ellen, at 148 Buckland Avenue in Dover. They had a daughter, Edith, and nine sons, seven of whom were old enough to have served during the First World War. Their daughter, Edith, married one of her father's constables, Police Constable G.A. Merricks, on 10 August 1910, at the Congregational Church in Dover.

His second eldest son, Albert Edward Scutt, had followed in his father's footsteps and became a Police constable in the Dover Borough Police Force, on 13 October 1913. He enlisted in the Royal Field Artillery, on 14 June 1917, and became Gunner 631267 in the 10th Works Battalion. On 6 July 1918, he transferred to the Royal Garrison Artillery as Gunner 631267.

Walter Henry Scutt had been a railway booking clerk before the war before his war service. He married Ethel Amelia on 4 May 1918 at Tonbridge in Kent, and seven months later, on 7 December 1915, aged 21, he attested for general service at Canterbury, and was placed on the Army Reserve. He was not mobilized until 31 May 1918, becoming Gunner 209827 in the Royal Garrison Artillery. At the time he was living at 36 Athelstan Road, Faversham. He transferred to the Royal Engineers on 9 December 1918 and became Sapper 210539 and joined the 11th Transportation Stores Company. The beginning of the New Year saw him leaving for France, where he arrived on 3 January 1919. He returned to England on 24 October and the following week he was demobbed and placed on the Army Reserve on 1 November.

Ernest George Scutt enlisted on 13 July 1917 at Dover, then two weeks later he married Alice May Stainer on 26 July 1917 at Charlton-by-Dover. He was mobilized the following year on 5 January 1918. On his Attestation form he had put that his preference for the branch of the military in which he would like to serve, was the Royal Flying Corps. The next question on the form asked, 'Are you desirous of serving in the Royal Navy, if so, state your qualifications.' Ernest answered, 'Royal Naval Air Service', but he was allocated to the 1st Reserve (Garrison) Battalion, Suffolk Regiment at Gravesend, as Private 96877/52175.

It would appear that Ernest went absent without leave on 18

November 1918. On that day he left Dover en route to Sheerness when he reported sick, as this was the time when the inflenza pandemic was at its height perhaps he had caught the virus. He was admitted to Minster Military Hospital on the Isle of Sheppey, which is where he was last heard of. A letter was sent to the Commissioners of the City of London Police and the Metropolitan Police, as well as the Chief Constable of the Dover Borough Police Force, by the Suffolk Regiment, advising them that they were officially reporting Ernest as being absent without leave. His Army service record does not show when and how he was located, but he was demobbed on 6 March 1919 at Warley, Brentwood in Essex.

Charles Scutt's youngest Sydney Frank Scutt, was a Private (G/68587) in the Queen's (Royal West Surrey) Regiment. He was killed in action on 11 October 1918, just a month before the Armistice.

As for Charles, even though he had retired at the age of 50 in 1914 because of the injuries he had sustained earlier in his Police career, he passed away in September 1952 aged 88. His wife Ellen, survived him, but only by three months, passing away in December the same year. They had been husband and wife for sixty-five years, having married on 4 January 1887.

Special Constables

With all of the extra requirements that the Dover Borough Police had placed upon them during the First World War, they became reliant, to a certain degree, on Special Constables to help them fulfil their commitments. But it wasn't all plain sailing for this body of well-intentioned individuals.

In the early days of the war, armed Special Constables who had already been enrolled, were dispatched to guard the local waterworks and various railway bridges across the district, during the hours of darkness.

During the first week of the war there was a meeting of the Dover Watch Committee at St Margaret's Parish Hall, which included its president, Colonel Clay, who had previously been in command of the Ghurka Regiment, Captain Norman, Mr Roger Dawson and Mr Hugh Pennington. The committee felt unable to accede to the suggestion that had been made by the Chief Constable, Mr Fox, concerning the non-arming of Special Constables and what their duties should consist of.

On the evening of 21 August 1914 at a parish meeting at St Margaret's school, forty men were sworn in as Special Constables, as the demand for more and men for both the armed forces and policing purposes, continued to grow.

Ten days later on 31 August more Special Constables were sworn in by County Magistrates, Mr T.A. Terson and Mr J. Scott. They were:

Mr Sylvester John Bryant
Dr Chas H. Murphy
Mr William Sherwood Mockett
Mr Arthur William Green
Dr Charles Henry Adamson
Mr W.J. Todd (Captain)
Mr Victor G. Smith

Dr Allan Johnson Fairfax Clarke
Mr Anson Lewis Sumner
Mr A.T. Walmisley
Mr Thomas Basil Duguid
Dr Reginald Whistler Ord
Mr H.S. Cundell.

The following day, 1 September, saw a further three men added to the list:

Dr I. Howden
Mr T.B. Harby

Mr A.V. Edwards.

All of the men were earmarked to undertake driving courses and to work night shifts, carrying out mobile patrols of Dover, so that they could cover a much wider area and respond quickly to any situation which might arise.

Captain Norman had already agreed to give lectures about the current state of the war, every Monday evening at the parish hall. Previous lectures by him on the same topic had proved extremely popular with members of the local community, with the hall being crowded on each occasion. It was a strong indication that his words were resonating in the hearts and minds of the people in Dover, especially those who were of the wrong age to be able to enlist in the armed forces, but who still wanted to be of service to their king and country.

On 23 September a further group of men were sworn in as Special Constables for the Dover area, they were:

Lieutenant Colonel W.O. Cavenagh	Mr M. Hayward
Mr C.A. Greaves	Mr D. Bremner
Mr W.C. Downes	Mr W. Cocks
Mr R. Dawson	Mr G. Clark
Mr S.E. Sweatman	Mr W.N. Spinner

A meeting took place at the Temple Ewell parish hall on 1 October 1914. It was not well attended, even though two of the speakers were Admiral Frank Finnis and Colonel S.A.M. Montague-Bradley. Admiral Finnis emphasized that having control of the high seas was not ultimately going to win the war, and pointed out that no matter how strong and powerful the British Naval Fleet was, wars were always ultimately decided on the land, whether that be across the Channel in France or Belgium or on the home soil of Great Britain. Putting more men into the field than the enemy could, would ultimately lead to victory.

Colonel Montague-Bradley said that the way to ensure this was for the country to persuade its young men to enlist so that they could be sent across the English Channel to defeat the Germans who would not then be in a position to mount an invasion on Great Britain. A piece of scaremongering was included in his speech with the reminder of some of the atrocities which the German soldiers had, at that time, allegedly carried out. He continued to push home his point by adding that the possible horrors of an invasion of England by Germany, whose armies would, by their hatred of England, perpetrate atrocities far worse than they had so far on the continent.

At the end of the meeting, and one would assume as a result of the powerful and emotive speeches which had been delivered by the two men, especially Montague-Bradley's words, twenty men from the audience immediately stepped forward to volunteer for duty as Special Constables. They were:

Mr F. Finnis
Mr A.K. Mowll
Mr J. Friend
Mr T. Upton
Mr J. Macro
Mr C. Sharp
Mr A. Pain
Mr P.C. Wyborn
Mr E. Hutson
Mr G. Austin

Mr W. Waters
Mr A. Robinson
Mr T. Morrell
Mr H. Moore
Mr G. Dovey
Mr A. Johncock
Mr J. Bucktrout
Mr A. Hopper
Mr C. Groombridge
Mr A.J. Pain.

An article appeared in the *Dover Express* dated 9 October 1914, which included a list of all of those who had volunteered to become Special Constables throughout the Dover district. The list of names was as follows:

Mr F. Cotton-Stapleton
Mr C. Cotton-Stapleton
Mr G. Elliff
Mr J.B. Madge
Mr S. Houghton
Mr L. Dilnot
Mr H. Pennington
Mr C. Woodward
Mr S.T. Jell
Mr W.R. Moberly
Mr G. Moberly
Mr W.C. Wynn
Mr A.E. Wynn
Mr E. Goodban

Mr W. Copus
Mr C.H. Kenway
Mr S.H. Steward
Mr E. Curling
Mr J. Finnis
Mr S.P. West
Mr G. Chapman
Mr W. Goldsack
Mr R. Golder
Mr W. Heath
Mr G. Allen
Mr A.G. Edmond
Mr R.J. Knott.

The residents of the community of Temple Ewell had previously been accused of being 'slow in coming forward' in relation to providing men for the war and the more localized role of Special Constable. This issue had been well and truly addressed as a result of the parish meeting of 1 October when twenty men agreed to enrol in the Special Constabulary. This theme was continued two weeks later at a meeting on the evening of 15 October, when a further seven men from the parish volunteered to do the same, with all twenty-seven men being sworn in at the meeting by Sir William Cundell, JP. The additional seven men were:

Mr S. Franks
Mr H.S. Simpson
Mr H.G. Gambrill
Mr W.H. Maxted

Mr Hodgson
Mr G. Austin
Mr W. Marsh.

Some of the men who performed the role of Special Constable were so committed to the war effort, and not content with just being a Special, that they were also allowed by the Deputy Chief Constable of Kent, Captain H.E. Chapman, to enrol in the Volunteer Training Corps as well. This was permitted on the understanding that they were first and foremost a Special Constable, and as such would still be expected to be available at a moment's notice to deal with any call that was placed upon them by the Police.

As the policing commitments in Dover increased so did the need for even more men to undertake the role of Special Constable. Less than two weeks into the new year of 1915, a further thirty-four men were sworn in at the Dover Police Court, by four members of the Watch Committee, Mr M. Pepper, the Chairman, Mr G.C. Rubie, Captain R.B. Cay, RN, and Mr H. Hobday. They were:

Rev. W. Holyoak
Mr J. Cook
Mr E.H. Nye
Mr E. Grey
Mr J. Waller
Mr J. Redman
Mr T.H. Bales
Mr W. Turner

Mr S.E. Tupper
Mr W.S. Long
Mr J.G.B. Whorwell
Mr T. Page
Mr W.E. Heyman
Mr P. Howard
Mr G.H. Spinner.

A further thirty-four men were sworn in by Mr W.J. Palmer JP on 11 January. They were:

Mr C. Baker
Mr F. Chapling
Mr H. Petley
Mr A. Cook
Mr T. File
Mr T. Little
Mr E. Brown
Mr H. Smith
Mr A.J. Andrews
Mr F.W. Harman
Mr J.R. Nash
Mr E. Wells
Mr F. Pilcher
Mr E. Webb
Mr E. Pope
Mr C. Hogben
Mr W. May

Mr F.H. Iddenden
Mr C.S. Morris
Mr R.H. Baker
Mr A.E. Cullen
Mr J. Wells
Mr E. Brooks
Mr C. Wood
Mr T. Huntley
Mr A.W. Gilham
Mr R. Harvey
Mr M.D. Collard
Mr C. Beer
Mr J.B. Betts
Mr J.E. Williams
Mr H.T. Brewin
Mr P. Norris
Mr C. Ashdown

CHAPTER ELEVEN

Airfields of Dover

During the First World War, Dover truly was a hive of military activity. Part of this combined military might came in the form of three separate air bases, which were situated at the following locations: Gunstan Road, Swingate Downs and Marine Parade.

Gunstan Road, which was a Royal Navy Air Service aerodrome, was only open as a base for the duration of the war, and was closed in 1920. One of the aircraft that flew out of the base was a De Havilland DH9, with its twin cockpits. The area is today part of a local housing estate in the Dover.

The airfield at Swingate Down was a Royal Flying Corps Aerodrome, and was opened for the duration of the war, closing in its entirety by the end of 1920. Its original purpose in the early months of the war was as a landing area for aircraft to congregate before flying across the Channel to France. During the war it was also used as a training facility for new pilots as well as being a Home Defence base. Swingate was home to No.13 Reserve Squadron. No.62 Training Squadron took over in 1917 and the following year saw the airfield become No.53 Training Depot Station.

It was not until 1917 that Swingate had any real substance to it as far as its buildings went. Initially it consisted of a few wooden huts and hangers which did not suggest the airfield was meant to have a long term presence. But in 1917 the site acquired five large hangers to house its aircraft, as well as numerous other buildings, making life more comfortable for those who worked and lived there. These improvements spoke volumes about its newly acquired level of importance.

Swingate airfield saw numerous different aircraft take off and land during its existence, one of the more recognizable planes being the Blériot Experimental 2, or as it was more commonly referred to, the BE 2. The aircraft and its future variations were manufactured at the Vickers aircraft factory in Bristol and were one of the earliest used by the Royal Flying Corps.

BE 2c Aircraft

Other aircraft which flew out of Swingate during the war were the Sopwith Camels, which were a much sturdier aircraft than the BE 2 and were in service with the Royal Flying Corps between 1914 – 1916, and Avro 504s.

The Marine Parade location, was actually in Dover Harbour and was a sea plane station.

Sopwith Camel Aircraft

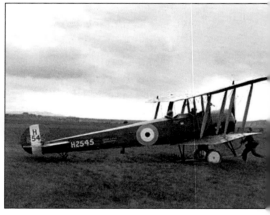

Avro 504 Aircraft

Memorial at Swingate

Aircraft from the Royal Flying Corps arrived in Dover on 3 August 1914, the day before war was declared. They arrived at Swingate Downs on what was simply an opened grassed field that had been roped off. Between 13 and 15 August Nos. 2, 3, 4 and 5 Squadrons flew out of Swingate and landed at Amiens in France in support of the British Expeditionary Force.

At Swingate there were no buildings at all to start with; no hangers for the aircraft, nor quarters for the pilots or mechanics and other ground staff, which just went to highlight the state of unreadinness that the country was in. There was also a neighbouring Royal Navy Air Service aerodrome.

After other aircraft had arrived during the following days, they then made their way across the English Channel before landing in France, on 13 August, in support of the British Expeditionary Force.

There was also an airship station at nearby Capel-le-Ferne, closer to the town of Folkestone than it was to Dover.

Besides all of the aircraft which flew out of these three locations, and the pilot training which took place at Swinton Downs, training was also provided for air observers, air gunners as well as radio techniques.

Sopwith Baby Camel

There were different types of aircraft that flew out of Dover. The Marine Parade location had Sopwith Baby Fight Seaplanes, which were mounted on floats and had front-facing machine guns. If the aircraft needed to be removed from the water for refuelling, repairs or general maintenance work, they were placed on a wheeled beaching trolley and manoeuvred on to dry land. These aircraft, and in fact all of the aircraft that were used at the Marine Parade station, had to be washed down with fresh water on a regular basis, to prevent some of their parts from corroding because of the continuous exposure to the salt in sea water. The Royal Navy Air Service also took over farmland that was situated at the rear of Fort Burgoyne, to provide them with a land based aerodrome.

The aerodrome at Swingate Down was home to No.50 Squadron which was established on 15 May 1916. Its pilots flew their first combat missions nearly three months later in August 1916 when they were involved in an attack on a German Zeppelin. The squadron saw continuous action throughout the war, as might be expected with their playing such an important role in home defence, protecting the skies over Kent and attempting to prevent German Zeppelins and Gotha aircraft from carrying out attacks on London.

It was one of the Home Defence Squadron's units that flew BE 12s as well as BE 2s, the latter, a twin-seater bi-plane, was used more as a reconnaissance aircraft, although some were subsequently converted into single-seater fighter planes with machine guns specifically used for attacking German Zeppelins. With the war at an end, the squadron was disbanded on 13 June 1919. Its commanding officer at the time was Major Arthur Travis Harris, who in the Second World War went on to become Air Chief Marshal Sir Arthur Travis Harris, and in February 1942, became head of Bomber Command. Known as 'Bomber' Harris, he courted controversy by employing the tactic of area bombing which resulted in the deaths of a large number of German civilians and the destruction of cities such as Dresden. It would be a further thirteen years before No.50 Squadron was reformed on 3 May 1937.

Many First World War pilots personalized their aircraft by adding paint designs to the sides, such as the ace of spades and the skull and cross bones or sweethearts' names emblazoned on the nose. With the life expectancy of pilots measured in minutes when engaged in combat with their German adversaries, it was an important aspect of what they did. Not all of the pilots were British; some were Canadians, some Australian, others South African and there were some from New Zealand. There were even American pilots, who before the United States entered the war in April 1917, had moved to Canada, so that they could join up.

As the war evolved, so did aircraft design. Collectively the Royal Flying Corps, the Royal Navy Air Service and latterly the Royal Air Force, used various different aircraft, as the role of flyers changed from being part of an observation platform in the sky, to being intelligence gathers who could go well behind enemy lines and unearth vital information that they otherwise would not have been able to discover. These were the type of roles that senior officers saw for their flyers. Initially they had no desire, will or intention to use them as an offensive instrument against the German aggressor.

At different times during the war aircraft that were based at airfields in Dover included, the BE 2, the BE 2c, the BE 12, the Bristol M1, the RE 8, the Armstrong Whitworth FK 8, the SE 5, Vickers FB 5 'Gunbus', Avro 504 RE 8, and the Sopwith Camel.

Out of the eight main cemeteries in Dover, only three of them have men who had been members of the Royal Flying Corps, Royal Navy Air Service or Royal Air Force, who are buried there. However, just because a British serviceman is buried in one of the town's cemeteries, does not mean that he was born in or has any connection with the town of Dover.

Air Mechanic 1st Class F/10461 George Saunders of the Royal Navy Air Service is buried at St Mary's New Cemetery. He died on 12 April 1916 aged 22. There are a total of twenty-nine men who served in the First World War buried in the cemetery.

He was part of the crew of HMS *City of London*, which started out as a small merchant ship, then became a balloon carrier, before being converted in to a seaplane carrier, which suggests a connection to the seaplane base at Marine Parade. His family home was at 284 London Road, Dover, Kent.

The 1911 Census confirms George's home address, and shows him living there with his parents, John and Alice Saunders, along with his elder brother, Herbert John Saunders, and his grandmother, Charlotte Mary Frith. The 1901 Census shows another brother, Alfred J. Saunders, who was twelve years older than George, and a younger sister, Clara Alice Saunders. Alfred enlisted in the Army on 11 November 1914 at St Paul's Churchyard in the City of London, and became a Private (3349) in the 3rd Battalion, Royal West Surrey Regiment, and at the time of his enlistment he was living at the Portland Hotel in London. He was appointed to the rank of lance corporal on 6 January 1915, acting corporal on 16 February, and acting sergeant on 20 March.

On 12 May he arrived in France, but three months later on 4 August he was back home in England. On 17 May he was promoted twice on the same day, first to the rank of a full corporal and then later the same day to sergeant. His pension record shows that less than four months after that, on 14 September 1915, he was discharged from the Army after having served for a total of 308 days, 'His service being no longer required', but there was no explanation as to why. The short period of time he spent serving in France strongly suggests that he was either wounded, or contracted an illness or disease that was debilitating, that he was no longer able to continue serving as a soldier.

I could find no record of his brother Herbert having served in the military during the war.

Charlton cemetery includes the graves of thirty-nine men who lost their lives in the First World War. Three of them were airmen.

Air Mechanic 2nd Class 141127 George Benjamin was only 19 when he died on 24 February 1919. He served with No.5 (Eastern) Squadron, Aircraft Repair Depot, which was first opened in May 1918 at RAF Henlow in Bedfordshire.

Edward Charles Hopper was born on 20 February 1893 in Dover. He enlisted in the Royal Naval Air Service on 27 May 1915 aged 22, rising to the rank of sergeant (205113) with his last date of service being 31 Mar 1918. He died on 25 February 1919 aged 26 and had previously been Mentioned in Despatches for his bravery earlier in the war. Before the war Edward was living at 50 Tower Hill, Dover, with his parents, Edward and Mary Ann Hopper, and his two younger brothers, Frederick Walter and Charles Frederick Hopper, both of whom were too young to have served in the war.

Harold Rosher was a Flight Lieutenant in the Royal Naval Air Service who died at Dover on 27 February 1916, suggesting that he was either involved in a flying accident or died as a result of illness, disease or wounds received in action. At the time of his death his home address was 40 Merton Hill Road, Wimbledon, Surrey. In his will he left the sum of £208 9s 9d to his brother, Francis Edwin Rosher.

St James's cemetery had 390 graves from the First World War, twenty-four of which were to men who either served with the Royal Flying Corps, the Royal Naval Air Service or the Royal Air Force.

Harold Carl Baker was a Canadian and a second lieutenant with No.49 Squadron, RFC. He died on 8 October 1916 at Dover as a result of injuries he had sustained in a flying accident. He was 20 years of age.

D.J. Barnes was from New Zealand and a second lieutenant with No.13 (Reserve) Squadron, when he died aged 22, on 24 July 1917.

Arthur Anderson Bishop was another Canadian pilot and a flight sub-lieutenant with the Royal Naval Air Service. He was killed in a flying accident at Dover on 14 September 1917, aged 22.

C.R. Bright was an air mechanic 1st Class (54499) with No.62 Training Squadron, when he died on 31 July 1917.

Clifford Edward Gordon Cooper was a South African and a second lieutenant with the No.62 Training Squadron, when he was killed in a flying accident at Dover on 26 November 1917. He was 19 years of age.

Henry Allen Edridge-Green, a lieutenant in the RAF stationed at the nearby Capel airship station, had previously served with the Royal Welsh Fusiliers. He died on 5 November 1918, just six days before the end of the war, aged 24.

F.S. Greatwood was a second lieutenant in the RAF and had previously served with the Royal Surrey Regiment. He was 23 when he drowned in the English Channel just off Dover on 12 April 1918. His name is one of those recorded on the Dover Patrol Memorial.

Clifford Robinson Hames, was a 23-year-old Canadian serving as a lieutenant with the RAF when he died on 25 April 1918.

John Bernard Hartnett was a Flight Sergeant (745) with No.49 Squadron, Royal Flying Corps, when he died on 23 January 1917.

A.W. Hofmeister was a second lieutenant in the RAF, and serving with No.53 Training Depot station when he died on 29 August 1918.

Leslie Sidney Hudson was a second lieutenant in the RFC, with No.49 Squadron, when he died on 27 October 1917. He was 21 and had previously served with the 1st Battalion, Gloucestershire Regiment.

William Barton Hughes was a lieutenant with the RFC, serving with 5th Group out of Dunkirk. He had qualified as a pilot in March 1917 and then went to work on a farm as a labourer until July 1917. He enlisted in the Royal Naval Air Service two months later in September. When the Royal Naval Air Service amalgamated with the Royal Flying Corps he became a pilot with the newly formed Royal Air Force on 3 April 1917. He was only 18 years of age when he died in a flying accident on 17 May 1918 at Dover.

At the relatively young age of 27, Douglas Hyde Hyde-Thomson was already a lieutenant colonel with the Royal Air Force Directorate of Air Organisation, when he died on 21 May 1918. He started his military career in the Royal Navy when, as a 13-year-old boy, he obtained a Naval Cadetship in August 1904. He went on to attend the Royal Naval College at Dartmouth as well as the one at Greenwich.

He then went on to serve on board numerous vessels within the Royal Navy, before carrying out important development work in the areas of torpedo-carrying aircraft along with wireless use by aircraft, both elements that were ground breaking work at the time.

He had flown to France on a visit of inspection at Dunkirk on 19 May 1918, and returned by air to Dover the following day. On 21 May he left by aircraft from Swingate Aerodrome about 9.30am en route to London. Soon after taking off he suffered engine failure and, losing engine speed, his aircraft nose-dived from a height of about 50 feet and crashed to the ground, a crash in which he sustained serious head injuries, from which he died half an hour later.

Letters sent to his grieving mother after his death showed the high esteem in which he was held by his fellow officers as well as his commanding officer. From their words it was clear to see that Hyde-Thomson was a truly remarkable individual who was innovative in his thinking and beliefs, a man who undoubtedly would have gone on to even greater achievements and been an asset to his country for years to come, had his life not been so cruelly extinguished at such a young age.

Thomas William Johnson was a 1st class air mechanic (7807) in No.52 Squadron, RAF. He died on 26 February 1919, aged 27.

James Frederick Hither was a second lieutenant in the RFC, No.62 Aerodrome and General List. He died on 12 December 1917.

H.M. Lee was a second lieutenant in the RFC and a member of No.62 Training Squadron, when he was killed on 26 September 1917, aged 24.

Raymond Sylvester Leventon was born in Huyton, Liverpool on 13 November 1898. In the First World War he became a second lieutenant in the RFC. He had learnt to fly in a French Caudron biplane at the Ruffy-Baumann School in Acton, London, acquiring his pilot's certificate on 23 June 1917. Just over four months later on 5 November 1917, and aged just 19, he was dead, having drowned in a flying accident over the North Sea. His records show that he was serving with No.49 Squadron, which was formed at Swingate on 15 March 1916 and remained there until 12 November 1917, when they flew out to La Bellevue in France.

Roderick Oswald Corderoy MacDonald MC MiD was a captain in

the Royal Air Force with No.53 Training Depot Station at Swingate. His parents lived at Norman House, St Margaret's, Dover. He began the war as a second lieutenant into the Royal Field Artillery on 15 August 1914. His MC was gazetted in September 1916 when he was a lieutenant with the RFA for 'conspicuous gallantry in connection with the registration of his own and other batteries of the brigade. His duties often took him out in front of our own troops. He carried out his work with extraordinary determination and at great personal risk.'

J.W. Mart was a sergeant (202660) in the 14th Balloon Battalion in Hythe. He died on 28 May 1919.

R.J. Moore was a second lieutenant in the RFC No.62 Training Squadron, when he died on 7 November 1917.

William Smith Oliver was a Canadian born on 26 July 1891 in Toronto. Although living in Calgary, Alberta at the time, he travelled all the way to St Antonio in Texas to qualify as a pilot, crossing into America on 16 January 1916. He travelled across the country and attended the Stinson Aviation School and learnt how to fly in a Wright biplane, passing out on 22 March 1916. Some time after this William travelled to England and enlisted in the Royal Naval Air Service as a pilot with the rank of flight sub-lieutenant and was stationed at Dunkirk. He was killed in a flying accident on 24 March 1917.

Victor George Osterroth was a Private (E/906) with D Company, 27th Battalion, Royal Fusiliers, but attached to the RFC, when he died on 24 January 1916 at a military hospital in Dover. He was 24 years of age and it would appear that his death was the result of an accident. Prior to the war he had been an insurance clerk living at 12 Colberg Place, Stamford Hill, London, with his mother, two elder brothers and a younger sister. He left £213 3s 9d in his will to his widow, Mary Ann Matilda Osterroth.

John Wilson Tailford was originally from Northumberland, born in Tynemouth on 6 March 1893. He volunteered for active service at the outbreak of the First World War and was commissioned into the 7th (Service) Battalion the Border Regiment in September 1914 as a second lieutenant. He was promoted to the rank of lieutenant two months later in November, and was further promoted to the rank of captain April 1915. He arrived in France in July 1915 and was subsequently wounded on three occasions. He qualified as a pilot in

September 1916 and was promoted to flight commander on 21 May 1917, the day before he died in a flying accident in the skies over Dover.

He was awarded the Military Cross for a successful bombing raid behind German lines and was also recommended for the Victoria Cross by his colonel for leading a night reconnaissance mission, along with some Northumberland miners. As Tailford and his men were making their way across no man's land they came across a large number of German soldiers coming towards the British lines as part of a surprise attack. Tailford and his men started throwing grenades in among the unsuspecting Germans, killing a number of them. In the ensuing confusion, and in the midst of smoke, dust and noise and believing the British were upon them, the German soldiers started firing at each other, killing even more of their number. Tailford and his men made good their escape, returning to their own trenches, having thwarted what would have undoubtedly been a surprise attack on their own lines, and the loss of British lives. The award of the Victoria Cross was not approved.

On his death the general of the 17th Division, of which Tailford had been a member at the time of the action, wrote the following to his mother: 'When I commanded the 17th Division, his name was always being brought to my notice for acts of gallantry and self-sacrifice. You must feel proud at being the mother of such a hero as he was.'

A.A. Wilson-Walker was a second lieutenant in the RFC, when he was killed in a flying accident at 11.30am on 20 March 1916, when he was returning to the aerodrome at Duston. He appeared to be flying at a dangerously slow speed and as he went to turn the aircraft it nose-dived from an estimated height of 1,500 feet, smashing into the ground and breaking into pieces. Walker-Wilson was found dead still strapped into his seat. A post mortem discovered that he had a fractured spine and a fractured skull. Both of his legs and one of his arms were also broken. At the time of his death he had a total of sixteen hours flying time. He had previously served throughout the Gallipoli campaign. He was buried with full military honours and the band of the 6th Royal Fusiliers were in attendance, as were fellow officers and men from the Royal Flying Corps.

What was noticeable about a large percentage of the men who are buried at St James's Cemetery, is that they died not in battle at the hands of their enemy but through the unforeseen suddenness of tragic accidents.

CHAPTER TWELVE

Dover War Memorials

The Dover Town War Memorial was unveiled on 5 November 1924, by Vice Admiral Sir Roger Keyes. It initially recorded the names of 721 men from the town who were killed or died as a result of their involvement in the First World War. Over the years others have been added and the number has now reached 855.

There was not, and never has been, some official criteria that set out who could and couldn't have their names included on a town's war memorial. Most were paid for out of public donations and the decisions as to what it should look like and who would design and erect it, were down to a local war memorial committee. Most of those named would have been men who lived in and were born in the town. Some committees would opt to include those who were born in the town but had moved away, whilst others would include men who had not lived in the town for some years, but whose families did. A good example of this was Walter Daniel John Tull, who went on to become famous, not only as a professional footballer with both Tottenham Hotspur and Northampton Town, but as the first black officer

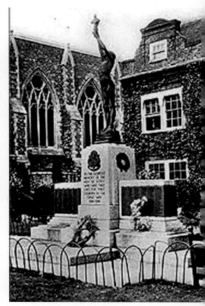

Dover Town War Memorial

in British military history to lead white men in battle. Walter was born in Folkestone and is rightly named on the town's war memorial, but he is also commemorated on Dover's war memorial.

The 1891 Census shows Walter, who was only two years old at the time, living with his parents, Daniel and Alice, his elder brothers, William (9) and Edward (4), and his sister Lelillia (7), at 50 Walton Road, Folkestone. Daniel and Alice had married in Elham, Kent in 1880. Alice died in 1895 aged 42, followed by Daniel who died two years later in 1897, when he was only 41. The only connection I could find for Walter and Dover was that his grandparents, on his mother's side, Stephen and Sarah Palmer, lived in Hougham, which is a village, parish and sub-district in Dover. Stephen was also born there. Stephen died in 1897 and Sarah died ten years later in 1907.

Walter Daniel John Tull

In the 1901 Census, Walter is shown as aged 12, living as an 'inmate' in a National Children's Home orphanage in Bethnal Green, in the impoverished East End of London.

By the time he was 21 in 1909 he was playing professional football for Tottenham Hotspur, for which he received a £10 signing on fee and a weekly wage of £4, which was a lot of money at the time. In 1911, after having made only twenty appearances for them, he was transferred to Northampton Town where he stayed until the beginning of the First World War, by which time he had played a total of 111 games for the club.

At the outbreak of the war Walter left behind his relatively safe existence to do his bit for the war effort like many other young men. So it was that in December 1914 he enlisted in the 17th Battalion of the Middlesex Regiment and, after having completed his basic training and spent time at different locations throughout the country, he finally arrived in France on 17 November 1915. He was subsequently promoted to the ranks of corporal and lance sergeant and in November 1916, he saw action during the Battle of the Ancre. In May the following year, he was commissioned as a second lieutenant in the 5th Battalion, Middlesex Regiment and was able to put his leadership skills to the test when he led his troops during the Battle of Messines in June 1917.

In December that year Tull and his men were sent to the Italian Front where they took part in the Battle of the River Piave. It was during this time that he was recommended for the Military Cross, an award that he was never given. After spending less than four months in Italy, Tull and his men were sent back to France in time to help to repel the German Spring Offensive which began in March 1918. It was during the Battle of Bapaume, near the village of Favreuil on 25 March 1918, whilst attached to the 23rd Battalion, Middlesex Regiment, that Walter Tull was killed in action. His body was never recovered, despite the brave efforts of one of his men, Private Billingham, to try and do so.

His name is commemorated on the Arras Memorial which is situated in the Pas de Calais region of France.

That Tull was promoted to the rank of lieutenant was an achievement in itself in the British Army of the First World War, where black soldiers outside of specific black units, such as the British West Indies Regiment, were few and far between. Most were used in a labouring role which saw them undertaking such menial chores as digging trenches or loading ammunition.

Whichever criteria was used for a war memorial there were always going to be at least three problems. Firstly, some names would be unintentionally omitted, especially in some of the bigger towns and cities, where thousands of men had gone off to fight in the war and the war memorial committees were heavily reliant on the friends and families of these men coming forward and letting them know of

their loved one's demise. Secondly, some towns and villages would record a man's surname followed by his initials, whilst others would use his complete name. Some would also record the man's rank and the regiment. The other issue was the recording of the names and the initials. These were not always recorded correctly, sometimes it might be down to just a single letter or an initial that had been either left out or engraved wrongly, but for

Walter Tull with two unknown fellow officers

those trying to trace a family member, this could prove extremely problematical.

War memorials are in some ways magical in what they stand for and the information which they provide for historians, relatives and future generations. They commemorate the names of the brave souls who, when called upon to stand up and defend their king and country, were, in most cases, prepared to do so willingly. Some did so out of honour and pride, whilst others saw it as their duty. There were even those who saw it as an adventure, but whatever their reasons were for fighting, those who are named on the war memorials up and down the country, ended up paying the ultimate price.

Abbot, A.S. S.

Ackehurst, A.W.

Addley, E.D.

Addley, S.

Ahern, L.J.

Ahern, W.

Alderson, A.E.

Allen, S.

Amos, A.E.

Amos, J.E.

Amos, R.

Andrews, C.R.

Andrews, G.W.

Andrews, H.R.

Andrews, R.S.

Arnold, W.J.

Ashman, C.W.

Atkins, H.R.

Attenborough, H.G.G.

Austen, F.

Austin, E.W.

Austin, J.J.

Back, C.H.

Back, J.R.

Bailey, B.J.

Bailey, E.

Bailey, E.T.

Bailey, F.C.

Baker, G.F.

Baker, G.H.

Baker, J.

Balding, F.

Baldry, A.H.

Ballard, T.J.

Banks, F.W.

Barber, G.J.

Barclay, E.W.

Barden, W.J.

Barker, W.J.

Barnard, S.H.

Barron, S.W.J.

Barstow, M.W.

Bartlett, C.F.

Barton, H.F.

Bartram, H.B.

Barwick, J.B.

Bates, G.
Bayard, A.R.R.
Bayley, J.T.
Bean, A.J.
Bean, W.E.C.
Beatty, H.G.
Becks, T.
Becks, W.J.
Bedwell, H.
Bedwell, T.W.
Beer, E.A.
Beer, W.T.
Beerling, A.L.
Beeston, R.C.
Belcher, J.
Bellfield, W.H.F.
Belsey, A.I.
Belson, G.L.
Berry, W.J.
Betts, J.E.W.
Bidgood, T.A.T.
Bingham, S.C.
Bish, E.T.
Bishop, F.G.
Bishop, W.J.
Black, N.V.
Blackett, W.S.B.
Blackford, W.J.
Blanche, W.E.T.
Bland, J.H.
Blatchford, J.W.
Blaxland, T.
Bligh, W.V.
Blogg, J.

Blundell, C.P.
Blythe, H.E.
Blythe, R.
Blythe, W.
Boakes, T.J.
Borrow, A.
Bourne, B.J
Bowlt, B.
Bowlt, F.W.
Bowman, A.M.
Boyton, V.H.T.
Brace, A.W.
Bradley, C.M.
Bradley, G.L.H.
Bradley, G.M.
Brand, B.J.
Brann, R.J
Breeze, A.R.
Brett, C.M.
Brewer, A.
Brice, G.F.
Brice, W.C.
Bridger, F.E.
Brightmore, H.
Brinkworth, J.W.
Broadbridge, L.A.
Brockman, A.
Bromley, C.P.J.
Brooks, S.J.
Brown, A.
Brown, G.A.
Brown, R.
Brown, V.
Brown, W.C.

Brown, W.J.
Browning, E.O.
Browning, T.J.
Bruce, H.K.
Brunton, E.W.
Burley, H.
Burnett, G.H.
Burrows, H.B.
Bushell, A.G.
Butcher, J.W.
Butler, R.H.
Butterfield, H.W.
Cadman, A.G.
Cairns, H.R.
Cannon, D.E.T.
Carey, L.A.
Carpenter, A.D.
Casey, H.T.
Caspall, P.R.
Cathcart, E.W.
Cave, H.J.
Cawtes, A.J.
Cay, A.L.
Chaddock, E.
Chandler, F.G.
Chandler, W.F.H.
Chapman, T.H.
Chase, H.C.
Chatwin, A.W.
Chettle, E.F.
Chidwick, J.T.
Church, W.
Churchill, C.H.M.
Clackett, C.

Clarett, F.G.
Claringbould, T.H.
Clark, F.H.
Clark, J.J.
Clark, P.J.
Clarke, W.
Claw, W.H.
Clifton, J.E.
Clitheroe, A.W.
Cloke, A.G. Cork, A.G.
Cohsall, J.
Cole, J.
Coleman, J.E.T. Cork, V.
Coleman, J.M.
Coley, W.J.
Collard, G.
Comper, E.J.
Cook, S.B.
Cook, W.
Cooke, C.F.
Cooke, F.
Cooke, F.
Cooke, H.
Cooke, T.G.
Coombe, E.B.
Coomber, H.
Coombs, E.G.C.
Cooper, A.E.
Coppard, F.A.
Cork, J.J.
Corteen, W.
Court, B.J.
Couzens, R.H.
Couzens, S.

Coveney, A.J.

Coveney, E.P.

Coventry, T.E.

Crascall, C.H.

Crascall, E.F.

Crepin, C.J.

Crockford, C.W.

Croft, R.J.J.

Crofts, E.L.

Crofts, W.F.

Croockewit, A.E.

Crutchfield, J.H.

Curd, W.A.

Curling, E.E.

Curtis, A.E.

Dadds, L.

Daniell, F.

Daniell, H.E.

Daniels, E.T.

Darwell, G.C.

Darwell, J.R.

Davidson, C.E.G

Davis, A.A.

Davis, A.B.

Davis, L.

Dawes, A.

Dawson, W.

Daynes, C.E.

Dearlove, A.W.

Dennett, T.S.

Dennis, C.G.

Dicks, S.D.

Diggings, F.W.

Dixon, E.E.

Dixon, P.

Dixon, R.J.

Dixon, R.J.

Dowle, R.J.

Dowle, W.R.

Draper, A.R.O.

Drew, E.J.

Dunbar, J.S.

Duncan, A.

Dunn, A.R.

Dunn, H.L.

Dunn, R.V.

Dunn, W.J.

Durban, A.E.

Dyer, A.H.M.

Dyer, E.G.

Dyer, S.A.

East, H.J.

Easterfield, G.

Eaves, A.T.

Edmond, E.J.

Edwards, A.

Edwards, F.W.

Ellender, A.G.

Ellender, R.A.

Ellis, C.E.

Ellis, E.B.

Ellis, G.A.

Erry, T.A.

Evans, A.W.

Evans, E.A.

Evans, V.S.

Everall, E.H.

Eversfield, T.

Faggetter, W.A.

Fairweather, W.H.

Farley, H.W.

Farrell, W.

Farrett, E.

Fennell, J.T.

Files, A.W.G.

Finn, T.G.

Fisher, R.H.

Fishwick, M.R.

Fleming, P.A.

Fogg, A.C.

Fogg, A.F.

Foreman, F.

Foreman, W.H.

Forth, W.S.

Foster, F.

Fowler, A.T.

Fox, J.C.

Frampton, W.J.G.S.

Franklin, R.

Franklin, T.

Franks, R.S.

Freeborn, A.E.

Freeman, C.W.C.

French, H.J.

Friend, J.B.

Friend, W.

Fry, H.

Fuller, W.E.

Fussell, W.

Fyrth, A.J.

Gabbe, A.C.G.

Gage, W.R.

Gale, L.F.

Gandy, F.R.G.

Gatehouse, E.W.

Gatehouse, W.J.

Gates, H.

Gates, T.J.G.

Geard, F.J.P.

Gibbons, R.G.

Gibbs, P.

Gilham, A.E.

Gill, T.H.

Gillham, F.H.

Glayzer, F.

Gleeson, A.

Godden, A.

Godden, H.

Godden, S.T.

Godfrey, C.W.

Golder, A.H.

Goldfinch, E.T.

Goldfinch, P.

Goldsack, E.J.

Goldsmith, H.

Goldstraw, G.P.

Goodburn, E.C.

Goodwin, F.G.

Gould, R.

Grace, W.H.

Grant, F.

Grant, H.A.

Graves, F.G.

Graves, H.K.

Gray, H.

Green, H.D.

Green, R.W.

Gregory, A.F.

Griffiths, J.T.

Griffiths, T.

Grigson, A.H.

Grigson, W.E.

Grounsell, F.C.

Hadlow, A.L.

Hall, F.

Hall, F.S.

Hamilton, J.

Hampton, A.

Handford, D.F.

Handley, W.E.

Hanson, J.

Hanwell, W.E.

Harbird, H.R.

Hardeman, E.T.

Harding, P.J.

Hardy, P.E.R.

Hare, A.J. J.

Harris, A.E.

Harris, A.J.

Harris, A.V.

Harrison, A.L.

Hart, H.

Hart, H.C.

Hart, H.P.

Hayes-Newington, C.W.

Hayward, H.

Hayward, J.H.

Hayward, S.P.

Hayward, W.

Head, W.D.

Hebden-Phillips, R.F.

Hedgecock, E.C.

Hedgecock, E.J.

Henderson, R.M.

Heron, A.E.

Hewes, E.A.

Hewes, H.G.

Hicks, H.C

Hickson, S.V.E

Hill, F.C.

Hobbs, R.

Hobbs, R.H

Hogben, W.J.N.

Holbrook, H.G.

Holden, G.S

Holderness, H.

Holland, H.E.

Holland, R.S.

Holmes, W.P.

Holyman, L.B.

Hood, C.R.

Hopkins, C.J.

Hopper, A.

Hopper, A.E.

Hopper, A.E.

Hopper, E.C.

Hosking, H.J.R.

Howard, D.B.

Howard, J.

Howard, R.

Howard, W.A.

Howell, S.G.S.

Hoy, E.G.

Hubbard, W.T.

Hudson, H.C.
Hughes, L.H.
Humphrey, C.
Hunter, T.
Huntley, G.
Husk, F.J.
Husk, H.J.
Hutchins, T.A.V
Igglesden, R.A.
Inwood, W.J.
Irving, C.R.
Irving, G.
Jackson, C.F.
Jackson, T.D.
Jardine, J.
Jarvest, A.J.
Jeffreys, F.W.
Jenner, W.C.
Johnson, F.
Johnson, J.
Johnson, M.W.
Jones, H.
Jones, T.E.
Jordan, G.H.
Keefe, J.
Keen, J.T.
Keighley, G.
Kemp, W.J.
Kennett, T.E.
Kennett, W.J.I.
Keyton, A.I.T.
King, C.
King, E.T.
King, T.E.

King, W.
Kingsford, A.C.
Kingsford, E.J.
Kingsnorth, C.
Kite, A.A.
Knell, L.W.
Knight, H.W.
Knott, H.R.W.
Knott, S.W.
Knott, T.J.
Laing, C.W.
Landall, H.H.
Laslett, W.S.B.
Laurie, A.W.
Laws, A.F.
Lee, S.G.
Leeds, F.J.
Letty, R.R.
Lewis, E.C.
Lewis, G.D.G.
Lewis, J.N.
Lewis, J.W.
Lewry, E.J.
Lilley, W.J.
Locke, G.E.
Loram, A.
Lovell, H.L-M
Mack, W.J.
Mackenzie, C.A.C.
MacWalter, C.C.
Magub, J.J.
Marbrook, A.R.
Marsh, A.J.
Marsh, C.

Marsh, E.A.

Marsh, G.A.

Marsh, J.T.

Marsh, P.

Marshall, H.G.E.

Martell, B.S.

Martin, G.

Martin, G.S.

Martin, J.

Martin, R.

Masters, N.D.

Matcham, J.R.

Matthews, H.S.

Maxted, P.J.

Maxted, W.J.G.

McCarthy, D.J.

McKay, A.J.

McLoughlin, F.

McMahon, J.P.

McNeir, G.A.

McPherson, D.

McPherson, H.F.

McTaggart, R.L.

Medhurst, F.

Mello, F.

Mello, P.F.

Mercer, E.C.

Metcalfe, J.W.

Mickle, F.W.

Middleton, G.J.

Millington, P.H.W.

Millne, C.H.

Mills, A.

Mills, J.A.

Mills, R.G.

Mills, W.A.

Minter, C.H.

Minter, E .W.

Mitchell, D.

Moat, A.E.

Morris, E.W.

Morris, R.

Morris, W.

Morris, W.H.F.

Morrison, A.H.

Morrison, R.G.

Morton, H.W.

Moss, B.

Moss, H.

Mowll, S.E.

Muddle, G.W.A.

Mutton, R.J.

Nash, A.J.

Nash, J.R.

Neill, C.S.

Newland, F.T.

Newman, J.W.

Newman, P.C.

Newman, R.H.

Newton, A.W.

Nicholas, H.C.

Nicholass, H.

Nimmo, A.C.

Norman, E.J.

Norris, F.J.

Norris, H.E.

Nowers, L.F.F.

O'Dell, G.A.

O'Lone, R.
Oliver, C.F.
Osborn, G.A.C.
Osborn, G.C.
Osborne, A.E.
Osborne, A.G.
Ovenden, H.
Packer, B.C.
Packer, E.W.
Pain, A.T.
Palmer, G.T.
Palmer, S.J.A.
Palmer, T.W.
Parker, A.G.
Parker, D.
Parker, G.W.G.
Parsons, E.S.
Parsons, R.S.
Parsons, S.J.
Pearce, G.T.
Perry-Ayscough, H.G.C.
Pettet, W.H.
Petticrew, A
Phillips, O.
Phipps, C.
Phipps, C.
Phipps, E.
Phipps, E.W.
Phipps, F.E.
Phipps, J.W.
Phipps, W.R.
Piddington, W.T.
Pierce, A.C.H.
Pierce, A.E.

Pierce, A.E.
Pierce, S.
Piggott, H.
Piggott, H.W.
Pilcher, C.
Pilcher, G.H.
Pinks, D.S.
Piper, T.W.H.
Podevin, G.S.
Port, A.G.
Port, C.W.
Pott, D.R.B.
Potter, E.E.
Potter, M.W.
Potter, S.W.
Powell, R.G.
Prescott, R.
Prescott, R.H.
Priest, A.
Pullen, E.
Purser, F.C.
Rawlings, G.
Raysbrook, E.A.
Reader, F.
Reader, P.S.
Reader, R.E.
Redgate, G.W.
Reeder, R.
Reeve, W.D.A.
Reeves, E.
Reeves, M.B.
Reid, A.V.
Rich, F.
Richards, E.J.

Richardson, C.W.

Richardson, E.

Richardson, R.J.

Richardson, W.A.

Riches, W.V.

Rigden, G.

Roberts, A.H.

Roberts, I.

Robinson, C.E.B.

Robinson, H.P.

Rogers, G.

Rouse, A.C.

Russell, H.

Sabey, F.

Sait, A.G.R.

Sambrook, C.D.J.

Samways, A.H.

Sandham, L.H.

Sarsons, J.A.G.

Saunders, G.

Saunders, J.B.

Saunders, L.T.

Saunders, W.

Savage, F.W.

Sayers, J.B.

Scarlett, E.

Scott, A.

Scott, D.

Scutt, S.F.

Sedgewick, C.

Sedgewick, E.C.

Sedgwick, E.

Sedgwick, F.

Sedgwick, F.

Sedgwick, F.

Sergeant, F.W.B

Sergeant, H.V.

Sharman, H.

Sharp, E.A.

Sharp, E.S.H.

Sharp, S.E.C.

Sheppard, F.A.S.

Sherren, A.O.

Sherren, H.G.

Shillito, W.H.

Shingleton, A.R.

Shott, H.H.

Sidders, H.F.

Sidders, J.J.

Siffleet, A.L.

Simmonds, G.H.

Simmons, C.D.

Simmons, H.

Simmons, J.H.

Simpson, D.P.T.

Skiggs, V.J.

Smart, G.H.

Smith, A.

Smith, C.

Smith, C.

Smith, F.W.

Smith, G.A.

Smith, J.W.

Smith, T.J.

Smith, W.T.

Smith, W.T.

Snelling, A.H.

Sole, E.W.

Sole, F.H.
Sole, W.H.D.
Solley, E.W.
Southen, W.R.
Spain, A.
Spain, E.S.S.
Spain, T.E.
Spendiff, W.G.
Spendiff, W.S.G.
Spinner, W.G.
Spittle, R.G.
Squibb, H.
Squire, B.B.
Stageman, J.
Stamp, C.
Stanbridge, R.M.
Stanley, L.G.
Statham, H.K.L.
Stephenson, P.S.
Stevens, A.R
Stevens, A.R.
Stevens, E.P.
Stevens, G.V.
Stevens, H.
Stewart, A.W.
Stewart, H.W.
Stewart, J.A.
Stilwell, M.J.
Stitson, F.
Stokes, C.
Stokes, F.J.
Stokes, H.
Stokes, L.L.
Strand, H.

Streat, C.W.
Stubbs, W.C.
Sturges, A.
Sumner, D.C.
Swaby, C.
Symes, P.B.
Taylor, J.
Terry, H.
Terry, S.J.
Tester, A.E.
Tester, H.
Thomas, E.W.
Thompson, F.C.
Thompson, J.J.B.
Thompson, S.A.
Thorner, R.E.
Thorp, A.T.
Thurley, C.A.
Tierney, M.P.
Tiltman, A.V.
Todd, E.
Torr, D.K.
Tucker, H.B.
Tugwell, C.
Tull, W.D.J.
Tunnell, O.
Turner, B.A.
Turrell, G.
Upton, H.
Upton, L.H.
Usherwood, H.C.
Vale, F.J.
Valentine, W.G.
Vanson, R.W.

Vidler, A.E.
Vigor, C.J.
Waight, J.H.
Wall, T.W.
Waller, P.J.
Walsh, P.J.
Walter, E.J.
Ward, S.G.
Waters, W.
Watson, A.V.C.
Watson, F.
Watson, G.
Watson, R.C.
Watts, A.H.
Watts, W.E.A.
Wayte, J.N.
Webb, H.C.
Welch, D.
Wellard, G.J.
Wells, A.J.
Wells, E.
West, W.
Whiles, T.P.
Whiteman, E.G.
Wickes, T.R.E.
Wickham, C.E.
Wickham, F.
Wickham, W.E.
Wicks, A.G.

Wicks, T.
Wiley, W.
Williams, G.E.J
Williams, W.H.
Williams, W.S.S.
Willis, A.
Willis, H.
Wills, A.C.
Willson, A.J.
Wilshire, C.E.
Wilson, C.E.
Wilson, H.P.
Winkworth, E.J.
Wise, J.
Wood, C.E.
Wood, J.F.
Wood, J.T.
Wood, W.
Worster, A.F.
Worster, D.F.
Wyborn, D.
Wyborn, J.F.
Wyborn, J.H.
Wynne, E.R.L.
Wynne, M.St-C. P.
Young, A.G.
Young, J.

When looking through that extensive list of names, there are brothers, cousins, fathers, sons, uncles, nephews who all fought and died for a common cause, the fight against a tyranny that wanted to dominate and take away the freedoms that all sovereign nations owned as a right. Instead they chose to fight for freedom and a better world for all.

A small number of them were professional soldiers who had already been in the military before the war began, but most of them were young men who had been plucked out of what was normality for them and sent off to fight in a bloody war in some foreign field. They were labourers, bus drivers, builders, miners, bankers, who all came from different spectrums of society, both the common man and the landed gentry alike.

Dover has numerous war memorials and rolls of honour that commemorate these fine young men. Some are from regiments who were stationed in the town, whilst some were businesses who wanted to remember members of their staff who had gone off to fight and who never came back. Numerous churches record the names of their parishioners who attended a service every Sunday morning, sitting in the same pews with their families, and who lost their lives on the battlefields of Europe and beyond. Public schools recorded the names of ex-pupils and masters who went off to fight and who sadly never came back.

The Dover Grammar School for Boys was founded in 1905 by Fred Whitehouse, who was also the school's first headmaster. Back then it was a mixed sex school and was situated at Ladywell in South East

Dover Grammar School for Boys 1917 Cadets

London. The school even had its own Army Cadets. The Dover County School, the name it was then known by, chose to remember the thirty-one former pupils who died as a result of the First World War, by means of a beautiful commemorative stained glass window, which also includes the following inscription:

'In honoured memory of old boys of the school who gave their lives for King and country in the Great War 1914 – 1919.'

The names of those thirty-one young men who are commemorated on the memorial, are as follows:

Barron, S.W.J.	Hardy, P.E.R.
Belson, G.L.	Holland, R.S
Broadbridge, L.	Hosking, H.J.R.
Brown, V.A.E.	Igglesden, R.A.
Coley, W.J.	Keightley, G.
Durban, A.E.	Knell, L.W.
Eaves, A.T.	MacWalter, C.C.
Ellender, R.A.	Magub, J.J.
Evans, A.W.	Minter, C.H.
Fishwick, M.R.	Parker, D.
Gates, T.J.C.	Reeder, R.
Gleeson, A.	Stewart, A.W.
Goldfinch, E.T.	Ward, R.H.P.
Goodwin, F.G.	Williams, G.E.J.
Graves, F.G.	Worster, A.F.
Hadlow, A.L.	

Dover Grammar School Honour Guard 1918

Dover College, which is situated at Effingham Crescent in Dover, was founded on 15 September 1871 by a group of local businessmen, who thought it a good idea for the town of Dover to have its own public school. Its first headmaster was Canon William Bell, which was very apt as the College sits in the grounds of a twelfth century Benedictine Priory.

At the beginning of the First World War the headmaster of the school was the Reverend Franklyn de Winton Lushington, but during the war he left the school and enlisted in the Army, becoming a captain in the Royal Army Chaplain's Department, attached to the Brigade of Guards; he arrived in France in 1915. From 18 September 1916, his home address was shown as being at 8 St Peter's Street, St Albans, Hertfordshire, but by the time he had applied for his wartime medals, his home address was The Vicarage, Danehill, Sussex.

The College also has a war memorial which commemorates those former pupils who died during the First World War. There are the names of 177 young men listed on that memorial. According to the College's website, during the First World War, fifty Old Dovorians were awarded the Distinguished Service Order, seventy-six were awarded the Military Cross, another 155 were Mentioned in Dispatches, and one ex pupil, Lieutenant Commander Arthur Leyland Harrison, Royal Navy, was posthumously awarded the Victoria Cross. The citation for his award was as follows:

'For most conspicuous gallantry at Zeebrugge on the night of 22nd-23rd April 1918. This officer was in immediate command of the Naval storming parties embarked on "Vindictive". Immediately before coming alongside the Mole Lieutenant-Commander Harrison was struck on the head by a fragment of shell which broke his jaw and knocked him senseless. Recovering consciousness he proceeded on to the Mole and took over command of his party, who were attacking the seaward end of the Mole. The silencing of the guns on the Mole head was of the first importance, and though in a position fully exposed to the enemy's machine gun fire, Lieutenant-Commander Harrison gathered his men together and led them to the attack. He was killed at the head of his men, all of whom were either killed or wounded. Lieutenant-Commander Harrison, though already seriously wounded and

undoubtedly in great pain, displayed indomitable resolution and
courage of the highest order in pressing his attack, knowing as
he did that any delay in silencing the guns might jeopardise the
main object of the expedition, ie, the blocking of the Zeebrugge-
Brugges Canal.'

He was an all-round sportsman. Whilst in the Navy he was capped
twice for England at Rugby Union, making him the only England
Rugby International, to have been awarded the Victoria Cross.

The Dover Patrol War Memorial commemorates
the names of the 1,702 brave young men who served
and died during the First World War, whilst serving
as a member of the Dover Patrol.

The Dover Patrol was a British Royal Navy
command force that had been tasked with guarding
the English Channel against the potential threat
posed by both ships and submarines of the German
Imperial Navy. In doing so they allowed much
needed food stuffs and other goods to arrive in the
United Kingdom, which in turn meant that both
the war effort and the morale of the people on the
home front could be sustained. The Dover Patrol
was also involved in ensuring the safe passage
of British troops and their equipment across the
English Channel, from ports such as Southampton
and Felixstowe.

Arthur Leyland Harrison VC

The memorial, the funds of which were raised
by public subscription, looks out over the English
Channel at St Margaret's-at-Cliffe, close to Dover, and was unveiled
by His Royal Highness the Prince of Wales, on 27 July 1921.

As can be seen in the photograph, most of the ladies are wearing
summer dresses without feeling the need for any kind of jacket or
coat, indicating that it would have been a reasonably good day weather
wise. The date of the unveiling was slightly unusual, as many of the
memorials across the United Kingdom were unveiled in the month of
November, coinciding with the annual remembrance service which
took place at that time of the year to commemorate the Armistice.

The inscription on the memorial reads as follows: 'To the glory of

God and in everlasting remembrance of the Dover Patrol 1914 – 1919. They died that we might live. May we be worthy of their sacrifice.'

There is also a hand written book of remembrance, which records the names of all the men who were killed whilst serving with the Patrol during the First World War. This is on view at nearby St Margaret's Parish Church.

The Dover Marine War Memorial commemorated the names of the men, who immediately before the outbreak of the First World War, had been working in some capacity for the South Eastern & Chatham Railway Company. In total 5,222 members of staff enlisted in His Majesty's armed forces during the course of the war, and 556 of them paid the ultimate price and never came home. It is these men's names that appear on the memorial.

Dover Patrol Memorial unveiling

The memorial is situated at what is now the Dover Cruise Centre at the Western Docks, but at the time it was the Dover Marine station. It was unveiled on 28 October 1922 by Mr R.H. Cosmo-Bonsor, who was Chairman of the South Eastern & Chatham Railway Managing Committee.

The station was opened on 2 January 1915 and was originally used as an Ambulance Train Railway for returning wounded soldiers. It remained in use as a railway station until the 1990s.

CHAPTER THIRTEEN

Post war Dover and Peace

With the signing of the Armistice on 11 November 1918 came the end of nearly four-and-a-half years of bloody and barbaric war, but it did not mean that everything would suddenly return to how it had been before the war; the world had now changed.

Worldwide, more than nine million military personnel and an estimated seven million civilians had died as a result of the First World War, with millions more wounded, many with life changing injuries.

The German Empire had been defeated and crumbled. There had already been a revolution in Russia in March 1917 which had seen the collapse of the Russian government. The Austro-Hungarian and Ottoman Empires no longer existed and France was left devastated. Most of the fighting that had taken place on the Western Front, did so on French soil. This resulted in large swathes of her countryside being destroyed, by miles and miles of trench systems, large bomb craters, and latent munitions making certain areas of land almost unusable. As a nation she had lost over a million of her young men killed, which was the highest percentage of men of those mobilized, of any of the major powers involved in the war.

France's government had to spend a small fortune to look after the millions of its wounded men who had returned home after the war, and the mental wards in its hospitals and asylums were full up with shell-shocked soldiers.

The Armistice brought rejoicing and celebrations in Dover as in every other village, town and city up and down the country, but initially there was no relaxing of pre-war restrictions, especially in and around the town's harbour. This included the Dover Barrage. A notice was placed in the press at the end of November to confirm that it had not been removed and to warn mariners to act only on official notifications regarding the sweepings of mined areas.

Celebrations were tempered due to the influenza epidemic which had struck the town. So bad had the matter become, that the week prior to the end of the war, Dover experienced a record number of funerals.

It was only after the German High Fleet and all her remaining submarines been surrendered to the British that the restrictions in Dover gradually began to be lifted. The town's people could at last walk unchallenged on the White Cliffs of Dover, and not have to fear being shot by a young and nervous soldier on sentry duty. The wartime lighting restrictions had also been abolished.

On Sunday, 17 November 1918, the Prince of Wales arrived in Dover, having been driven down from Buckingham Palace in London, so that he could meet and greet returning prisoners of war who had been held in camps throughout Germany. He was also there to pass on a message of thanks for a job well done and a welcome home on behalf of King George V.

There were 800 British prisoners of war who returned home on this day. Their vessel landed at Admiralty Pier. The sight of the large cheering crowds that greeted them, must have been an emotional experience. Some of these men had been held in captivity for more than four years, having not seen their loved ones in all of that time. Some of them had children they had either never seen or who they remembered only as babies.

The men were taken to the Great Hall at Marine station where they were inspected by the Prince of Wales as he walked amongst them chatting to them about their wartime experiences and their incarceration in Germany.

Sunday, 1 December 1918, at 11.30 am, saw the arrival of Marshal Foch in Dover, the commander-in-chief of the Allied armies, on his way to London. It wasn't a particularly good day to cross the English Channel. High winds and heavy rain would not have made for a pleasant crossing. He was in company with the French Premier, Monsieur M. Clemenceau, the Italian Prime Minister, Signor Vittorio Orlando and his Foreign Minister, Baron Sonnino also arrived in Dover at the same time.

Foch, who arrived aboard the French destroyer, the *Francis Garnier*, a Bouclier-class destroyer launched in October 1913, was originally due to sail into Folkestone, but because of the number of other French destroyers who would be escorting her, it was decided that Dover would be a better location, especially with the high winds and choppy seas at the time of the visit.

Vice Admiral Sir Roger Keyes, Lady Keyes and their three children were in Dover on 12 December, for him to be awarded the Honorary Freedom of the Borough at the Town Hall by the Mayor of Dover, for his services to both the town and his country, and a grand affair it was.

Haig and his generals arrive in Dover after the war

Just a week later on 19 December, Field Marshal Sir Douglas Haig arrived in Dover on his return from France. It was a triumphant return by a conquering hero, the streets were lined with thousands of well-wishers, adults and children alike, as the entourage of nine cars carried Haig and his generals through Dover to Marine station, where they were met by a group of distinguished guests which included the Lord Warden of the Cinque Ports, the Archbishop of Canterbury and the Mayor.

The Recorder of Dover read out the following address to Haig:

'We, the Mayor, Aldermen and Burgesses of the Cinque Port and Borough of Dover, desire, in welcoming you on your return

to England after the victorious termination of the hostilities in which the Empire has been engaged during the past four and a quarter years, to offer you our heartiest welcome and most cordial and respectful congratulations.

The splendid valour and unexampled endurance displayed by the British Armies in France and Belgium under your command, together with their deep devotion to their King and country, have afforded a glorious contribution to the successes collectively gained by the heroic Armies of the Allied and Associated Nations, and have nobly earned the gratitude and admiration of the civilised world.

From the loss at Mons in 1914 to its recapture on the closing day of hostilities, throughout all the changing fortunes of war, the high traditions, tenacity of purpose, and unyielding spirit of the British Army have ever been maintained. In our deep thankfulness to Almighty God, the Giver of all victories, we also beg to tender our sincere tribute to your most distinguished leadership and the invaluable services you have rendered to the Empire and the cause of freedom and humanity.'

It was interesting to note that there was not one word in the speech that mentioned the price which had been paid by the hundreds of thousands of young men who had lost their lives during the war, or of their families who had lost a loved one. Nor was there any mention of the hundreds of thousands of men who had been wounded, many with life changing injuries.

Haig replied expressing his thanks for the kind and heartfelt welcome that had been afforded to him and his generals. He also made mention of 'the wonderful men whose unique courage and endurance had at length brought them by victory to peace.' And with that he boarded his train for London.

Dover had become quite the celebrity town, unintentionally of course, but because it was the first port of call for those sailing to England from France, its name was in the newspapers on an almost daily basis.

The next visitor to arrive in Dover was the American President, Woodrow Wilson, who had been in France on the Western Front spending Christmas Day with some American soldiers. Even though the war had been over for some seven weeks the vessel he was sailing in, the SS *Brighton*, was escorted into Dover by the destroyer HMS *Termagant*, six other destroyers, twelve fast scouts, all from the Royal Navy, four sea planes and two big Handley Page bombers. The artillery battery at Dover Castle fired a salute as the *Brighton* entered the harbour. President Wilson and his wife were in England for five days before returning to France from Dover on New Year's Eve.

So after forty-two months of bloody and sometimes barbaric fighting, the war was at last over. Because Gavrilo Princip, a 19-year-old Bosnian, had murdered Archduke Franz Ferdinand of Austria and his wife, Sophie in Sarajevo, on 28 June 1914, some sixty million men had been mobilized into the military. An estimated eighteen million men, women and children had been killed. This included an estimated eleven million military personnel and seven million civilians. These figures included an estimated six million who had been reported as missing and whose bodies had never been found, and another two million who had died of illness and disease. Seven million military personnel were permanently disabled, with a further fifteen million who had been seriously injured.

The Ottoman Empire, and those of Austria-Hungary, German, and Russian, all ceased to exist by the end of the war. Poland became an independent country once again, and there were major changes in the Balkan countries, where the war had started.

After nearly four-and-a-half years of bloody conflict the war was finally at an end and peace once again descended on the warring nations. A war which had begun because of the deaths of one man and his wife, had ended in the deaths of millions more.

At a moment in time – 11am on 11 November 1918 – nobody could have foreseen what was to follow, after all, the ironically named Great War was supposed to be the war to end all wars.

Twenty years later, on the eve of the Second World War, it was obvious that lessons had not been learnt, either that or the memories of those dark days had simply faded too quickly.

Sources

www.1914-1918.invisionzone.com

www.cwgc.org

www.ancestry.co.uk

Wikipedia

Dartford and the Great War – R.B. Finch

Dartford & Folkestone during the Great War – Michael & Christine George

www.britishnewspaperarchive.com

www.roll-of-honour.com

www.naval-history.net

www.doverhistorian.com

www.historyplace.com

www.dreadnoughtproject.org

www.britishnavy.co.uk

www.wings-of-war.org

www.pastscape.org.uk

www.historypoints.org

www.libcom.org

Index